AN ICONOGRAPHER'S SKETCHBOOK:

DRAWINGS AND PATTERNS

Volume I, The Postnikov Collection

Translated and Edited by
Gregory Melnick

ST VLADIMIR'S SEMINARY PRESS
CRESTWOOD, NEW YORK

AN ICONOGRAPHER'S SKETCHBOOK:

Drawings and Patterns

Volume I, The Postnikov Collection

ST VLADIMIR'S SEMINARY PRESS

575 Scarsdale Road, Crestwood, New York 10707

1-800-204-2665 • www.svspress.com

The sketches were published originally as Переводы сь древнихъ иконъ изъ собранія А.М. Постникова. В. И. Успенскій, Издано при С. Петербургскомъ Археологическомъ Институтт. С. Петербург,ъ 1898.1898. Tracings from Antique Icons in the collection of A.M. Postnikov. V[asili] I [vaonovich]Uspensky, Published by the St Petersburg Archaeological Institute, St Petersburg, 1898.
And Древнія иконъ изъ собранія А.М. Постникова. М. И. и В. И. Успенскіе. Издано при С. П. Ъ. Археологическомъ Институтт. С. П. Ъ. 1899 Antique Icons in the Collection of A.M. Postnikov. M[ichael] I[cvanovich] and V[asili] I [vaonovich]Uspensky, Published by the St Petersburg Archaeological Institute, St Petersburg, 1898.

Cover by Copyright Grpahics, Lomita, California

ISBN 978-1-879038-10-3

TABLE OF CONTENTS

**90 Sketches from
"Tracings of Antique Icons in the Collection of A. M. Postnikov," 1898**

**98 Sketches from
"Antique Icons from the Collection of A. M. Postnikov," 1899**

PREFACE

The sketchbook you are holding is part of a collection of icon patternbooks produced by Oakwood Publications during the past ten years. They are designed to help meet the objective so well described by Bishop JOB in his presentation on "A Return to Basics" in Iconography:

"To be an iconographer, you must copy. To learn the tradition of iconography, you must simply copy initially. You will never go wrong if you copy a good model. Eventually the Holy Spirit adds to your skill and experience and then you will develop your own 'style.' This 'style' is the product of prayer and study, the painting of many icons, and obedience to the tradition. It doesn't sprout full formed with your first icons."[1] Bishop JOB went on to describe the basic elements of Beauty, Harmony and Truth (or Virtue) which should be present in all icons produced as prayerful objects and not as desirable *objets d'art*. Bishop JOB concluded his presentation with the following: "Your eye is the lamp of your body, when your eye is sound your whole body is filled with light, but when it is not sound your body is filled with darkness' (Matt. 6:22-23). Light is given to us by the holy icons, therefore, it is good for us to come to the icons for spiritual enlightenment. From the icons we receive joy that is shown through their colors as well as knowledge about God and His saints."

Gregory Melnick, with these two volumes of "new" icon patterns, has again produced a masterpiece of expertise designed to support the work of icon painters and others interested in authentic iconography. Mr. Melnick, an ordained reader in the Orthodox Church, is a translator *par excellence*. He has previously produced *An Iconpainter's Notebook* with a wealth of narrative information on hundreds of icon patterns. His expertise and knowledge in Slavonic liturgical arts permit him to furnish not only a translation of the titles of the icons presented in these volumes, but a wealth of information about the context of the icons, their history, design, religious significance, etc.

We are very pleased to be part of his and others' efforts in our quest to make known to all the beauty and depth of authentic iconography in all its liturgical aspects.

Philip Tamoush, Publisher.

---

[1] This and the following quotations are from the "Keynote Address" of Bishop JOB of Chicago, Spiritual Adviser to the St. John of Damascus Association of Orthodox Iconographers, Iconologists and Architects, at its 1966 Annual Meeting in St. Charles, Illinois, printed in the *Sacred Arts Journal*, Volume 17, Number 2, Transfiguration, 1996.

FOREWORD
by Karyl Knee

Again, Oakwood Publications has provided iconographers with a valuable tool to expand and enhance their knowledge of icons. This publication is essential for iconpainters and students of iconography to be able to draw on. Having these works in English enables the iconpainter to have more icon models to guide him and is enhanced by experienced iconographer Gregory Melnick's comments.

Gregory Melnick also translated and edited the "Bolshakov" text to the *Stroganov Iconpainter's Patternbook* and with these present icon tracings, selected by their Russian collectors, greatly expands the scope of the English-speaking iconographer into new icon compositions in addition to the calendar presentations in the *Stroganov Patternbook*.

Publications of this kind were instrumental in the promotion of interest and knowledge of icons and iconography, and date from the beginning as popular interest in this essentially religious art form. It is from material such as this that the Russian and western populations came to realize the beauty and spirituality of icons.

These tracings of the A. M. Postnikov, I. V. and M. V. Tyulin icon collections were made by two Uspensky brothers at the turn of the century. The works were published by the St. Petersburg Church Archaeological Institute which, along with its distinguished director Nikolai Vasilevich Pokrovsky, produced much material on icons and iconography.

There were three Uspensky brothers, Michael Ivanovich, Vasili Ivanovich and Alexander Ivanovich, along with a sister Yu. Ivanova Uspensky. The St. Petersburg Church Archaeological Institute publications also mention a D. Iv. and an I. Iv. Uspensky, but it is not known if these last two were members of this particular Uspensky family, although the Institute lists them as contributing authors.

The Uspenskys were from the Tula Province of Russia and in keeping with the educated people of their time, they were experts in many areas. In this case they all were experts in the areas of archaeology, history, religion, education, ethnology, geography and geology. They all distinguished themselves in the areas of archaeology and the history of Russian art, publishing articles from 1898 on.

In the back of a 1900 publication of the Uspensky's Tyulin Collection tracings, the Church Archaeological Institute lists the authors' works and some background on them. They list Michael as being at the Voronezh Seminary School, Vasili as being with the St. Petersburg Archaeological Institute, and Alexander as being the Moscow Archive Minister at the Imperial Palace. They also list D. Iv. and I. Iv. Uspensky as being at the Tula Province Bureau.

Michael was born on October 26, 1866 in the Tula region. He attended the Moscow Institute where he studied archaeology and the history of Byzantine art. He published works on a variety of subjects: mathematics (1899), elementary education (1908) and mines and metallurgy (1931).

In 1899 and 1900 Michael collaborated with his brother Vasili on three of the works included in this new two-volume edition. In 1901, again with Vasili, he published *Notes on Ancient Russian Iconography* about the early icon painters, St. Alipy of the Kievan Caves Monastery and St. Andrew Rublev.

In 1922, when Michael was 56 and his youngest brother, Alexander 49, they founded the Institute of Archaeology in Moscow where Michael held the chair in Archaeology from 1922 - 1928. Michael was also a Professor of Western and Eastern Art at the University of Leningrad from 1923 to 1928. From 1928 to 1931 he was at the Central Bureau of Regional Studies. He died at the siege of Leningrad on November 9, 1942.

Not much is known about the middle brother, Vasili. Some libraries give his birth and death date as the same as Michael's, but biographies of the time do not mention that he was Michael's twin brother, and one French biographical work lists his name as "Vladimir." In 1900 he was at the St. Petersburg Archaeological Institute where he wrote one of the books in this present set as early as 1898 and co-wrote many books on icons and iconography with his brother Michael.

Alexander, who attended the University of Kharkov and qualified as a private docent for the Chair of History and Art, was an even more prolific writer on icons and iconography.

By 1900 Alexander began publishing a three-volume work on icons at the Church Archaeological Museum and in 1901 a work on Simon Ushakov's icons in Moscow. Alexander was also the editor of Sergei Bolshakov's 1903 edition of the *Stroganov Iconpainter's Patternbook*. He also supervised activities in numerous provinces in Russia. He died in 1938.

Their sister, Yu. Ivanova, is credited with work regarding Old-Russian Art and a catalogue of Pushkin's home as late as 1946.

The modern iconographer should be very grateful for this talented family's work.

INTRODUCTION

I wish I had this set of "Sketchbooks" thirty years ago. In the 1960's it was difficult to find suitable patterns and models for icons which frustrated designing "original" icons. Here at last are 198 tracings of antique Russian icons that are not the famous "classics" found in all the albums of Russian icons, but rather represent iconography as it was known at the end of the nineteenth century when there was a movement to return to basics. At that time there was a great flowering in Russia of encyclopedic works on Orthodox liturgics and spiritual literature.[2] Except for some of the work done in the "painters' villages" of Palekh and others, Russian iconography was western European in concept and execution. The transition from the "Eastern" or "Byzantine" to the "Western" style was gradual but complete from the time of Peter the Great until World War II. The refined European taste of high society in the "new" capital, St. Petersburg, was the model and ideal for the decoration of churches throughout the Russian Empire. In the great cathedrals, monasteries, parish churches and in believers' homes with few exceptions the icons were western. The old icons were often painted over in the modern style. Even today almost all of the older generation of pious Russian Orthodox expect icons to be as realistic and pretty as they remember them in the Old Country. They simply do not like the old Russian icons (or the new Russian icons painted like the old ones either) and do not want to learn to like them. They perceive the genuine and traditional Orthodox icons to be distorted and ugly. This includes the sublime works such as St. Andrew Rublev's "Holy Trinity" and the "Vladimir Mother of God." This prejudice is difficult to overcome because the spiritual reality represented in Orthodox icons is difficult to explain. Genuine icons have the same spirit and feeling as the Gospel; at once simple, yet otherworldly. There is nothing sentimental or adapted to our expectations or demands. However, when we adapt ourselves to the spirit of the Gospel, the icons reveal themselves in their truth and clarity. Those who cling to pretty and sweet western paintings and reject genuine icons miss something essential to Orthodoxy. The merely physically beautiful and realistic paintings evoke shallow emotions in people who mistake pious feelings for spirituality. This is a tragedy, and not merely a matter of aesthetic sensitivities.

At the beginning of the twentieth century people did not know what classic Russian icons looked like. The genuine icons were not accessible to the vast majority of believers because old icons were painted over with new icons over the course of time as the "olifa" varnish darkened. Other icons were "locked away" in royal churches and chapels that were not open to the public. A mistaken form of piety covered the most sacred and miracle working icons with elaborate and jeweled covers which prevented people from seeing more than the faces and hands. The great iconostases more often than

---

[2] I have in mind the monumental works of Dyachenko, Bulgakov, Nikolsky, Skaballanovich, etc.

not appeared as great ornate walls made of polished silver and gold with the small painted areas appearing as black "ink blots." Fortunately there were individuals who rediscovered the beauty of traditional Russian icons under the metal covers and dark varnishes, among whom are the personages responsible for the tracings in this book. That the original editions of the Postnikov and Tyulin books were limited to fifty copies is evidence of the number of individuals at the turn of the century who would be interested in purchasing books of traditional iconography.

The original plan of Oakwood Publications was to make facsimile editions of the four Postnikov and Tyulin books. It has since been discovered that facsimile editions of these works are being made available by other publishers principally in Russia. After considering various possibilities, it was decided that it would be best to redo the books completely, "translate" them if you will, to make the drawings more accessible. There is no text or explanations in the originals apart from the Russian titles repeated in the table of contents. The original books are ponderous and hard to store. The drawings and tracings in the originals are very difficult to appreciate since they are printed in reverse; that is, as a mirror image. There is, of course, a reason for this. Iconographers in the iconpainting villages and workshops in past centuries produced icons in the assembly line method, each craftsman doing a single operation: one did the priming, one the garments, another the faces, still another the lettering, etc. They used to make "editions" of perhaps fifty of each icon. Since it is very tedious to trace, and a paper pattern will tear if traced fifty times, the master iconographer drew his designs in reverse, then pricked tiny holes in the paper through which he forced powdered charcoal to form the outline of the design on the prepared panel, which was then incised and painted as usual. It is obvious the charcoal would blacken the design side. Today an iconographer does not paint the same icon fifty times and normally does everything himself. One person can hardly master all of the various skills required so modern icons cannot be compared to the technically perfect icons produced by teams of specialists.

These drawings in these volumes are not designs for icons. The original drawings were done by several artists with varying ability and since the width or thickness of the lines in the drawings varies, some of the patterns did not reproduce well. This will not be a problem, since the designs must be redrawn anyway to produce a new icon. The *Sketchbooks* are therefore presented as "idea" or "studio" books. It is assumed that iconographers have other resources at their disposal. I recommend that these volumes be used in conjunction with *An Iconographer's Patternbook: The Stroganov Tradition, An Icon Painter's Notebook: the Bolshakov Edition, The Icon: Image of the Invisible, The Image of God the Father* together with other books of traditional Russian Orthodox icons. The descriptions in *An Icon Painter's Notebook* frequently refers to other saints as models, such as St. Blaise, for instance. Most of these "model" saints are represented in this set.

It is with fear and trembling that one puts his hand to translate and correct expressions of Orthodox Tradition. Regretfully, a few illustrations are very poorly drawn while a few others are not expressions of Orthodox teaching. This is mentioned in the Commentary. However, some of the design elements in these drawings are valuable, such as the symbols of the evangelists, and so they have been reprinted. Nothing in the original editions has been left out of this edition.

The Commentary section explains the illustrations with a few hints for icongraphers. A few obscure words and technical terms are in the Glossary. All of the names of saints in group icons except for "The Miracle Workers of Novgorod" are listed individually in the Index.

I would like to thank A. Charles Kovacs for reducing the drawings to a manageable size and Karyl Knee for the Forward, for supplying missing drawings and for the use of her manuscript index to illustrations of icons.[3] All of their suggestions have been useful. Most of all, I would like to thank Philip Tamoush for encouraging me by his dedication to Orthodox iconography.

Having painted icons since 1961 when there were so few pictures of icons available, and knowing how difficult it is to design "original" icons, I sincerely hope this new edition of the Postnikov and Tyulin Collections[4] will be an inspiration to my fellow icon painters and aid the painting of modern traditional Orthodox icons.

Gregory Melnick
Syracuse, New York
February, 1997.

---

[3] *An Icon Source Book*, Oakwood Publications, 1997.

[4] *An Iconographer's Sketchbook Volume I* contains the two volumes of the Postnikov Collections. *An Iconographer's Sketchbook Volume II* contains the two volumes of the Tyulin Collections, published separately.

An Iconographer's Sketchbook Vol. 1

THE POSTNIKOV COLLECTION

THE original Postnikov editions do not have any text except the captions on the sketches. The notes are newly compiled for the Oakwood Publications edition. They are intended to identify the icons and to give a transcription and translation of the inscriptions. All of the original drawings are reproduced here. I ascribe the anomalies in the drawings to the enthusiasm of the artists and collectors to the whole new world of Russian iconography that they were re-discovering at the end of the nineteenth century. There are comments about inappropriate icons throughout these volumes. I am presenting iconography as it is *in reality*. I do not approve of, nor wish to perpetuate heresies or bad iconography. Details in these sketches can be very valuable for the design of new icons. For example, someone might need an elegant design for a miter, or wings, or crossed hands or decorated robes. It would be a great loss to omit "The Savior 'Blessed Silence'" Sketch 1:14 because it is an example of confusing symbolism. Originally the sketches were published as a mirror image. The drawings have been reversed by me and appear "correct." However, unfortunately a number of drawings have inconsistencies. For example, lettering may be both correct and reversed in the same drawing. I did not write commentaries on well-known icons which are explained in many other excellent books on iconography. Specific information on a topic is not always given in the first entry; other entries can be found in the Index.

To avoid repeating the same information in almost every entry the following information is assumed for each sketch: Icons of our Lord Jesus Christ have His Name abbreviated as "ıc̄ x̄c̄" which are the first and last letters of the Greek Ἰησοῦς Χριστός written in Slavonic letters. His halo has a three-part cross on which are the letters "o ѽн" which is Greek ὁ ὤν for "THE BEING" or "I AM" written in Slavonic.[1] Icons of the most holy Mother of God have her name in Greek Μήτηρ τοῦ Θεοῦ abbreviated "м҃р ҙ҃.в҃." Generally, in this text, "Богородица" is translated "Theotokos" and "Богоматерь" as "Mother of God." Many icons of the saints are inscribed with the Greek word for "saint" ὁ ἅγιος instead of the Slavonic ст҃ый. "The angel of the Lord" translates а́гг҃ела г҃днь or а҃ г҃. As in the church service books, only the first letter is capitalized; in Slavonic the abbreviations are the sign of respect.

---

[1] The icons should have "ѡ̈" instead of "ѿ." See *An Icon Painter's Notebook*, page 44.

The English titles of the sketches generally are translations of the Russian captions which are reprinted in a modern civil typeface. These are followed by the Slavonic titles and texts transcribed in a modern Church Slavonic typeface. The Slavonic texts are transcribed and translated independently of the Russian title. The old icons were not inscribed in the standardized Church Slavonic "of the printed books" in which modern icons are usually inscribed. The script on the icons is very often calligraphic with unusual abbreviations and without spaces between the words. However, the inscriptions are generally consistent and it appears the iconographers copied them very carefully from existing icons or from their manuscript pattern books. Every tradition was considered something so sacred that it could not be "touched," even if an error were obviously a handwriting mistake. A number of errors from the manuscript tradition are still found in modern westernized icons. A "|" marks a division in a text. [My additions to texts and conjectures are enclosed in brackets.] In viewing the sketches the following convention must be kept in mind: the lines that form the design are black, but the black patches represent a "bright" area or highlights. The lettering is "bright" red on gold; or perhaps gold or white on a dark color. Originally some sketches had the highlights printed in red ink which did not reproduce well. The sketches are greatly reduced in size from the originals. To avoid losing the fine lines, they appear "blacker" than the original drawings. The colors and additional information for many of the sketches can be found in *An Icon Painter's Notebook* and *An Iconographer's Patternbook* according to the day of the church year starting in September.

TRACINGS OF ANTIQUE ICONS

1. **The Image of the Most Holy Theotokos "Sweet-Sorrow"**
    Образъ Пресв. Богор. Умиленіе
    Ѻ҆бразъ прест҃ы́ѧ бц҃ы оу҆милє́нїе

The word *"Umilenie"* is difficult to translate. It means heart-broken, or humble, or sorrowful, but sometimes also tender, or it can also describe a very delicate spiritual feeling. The Slavonic word also translates a Greek word that the New King James Version translates sometimes as "confusion." There are different icons of the Mother of God in this collection named *Umilenie*. In fact, icons are not inscribed with this name and it is possible that "Sweet-Sorrow" is a generic name for icons whose title and feast day are not known.

2. **The "Vladimir" Icon of the Mother of God**
    Владимірская Икона Богоматери
    Ѻ҆бразъ прест҃ы́ѧ бц҃ы влади́мїрскїѧ

This is one of the most famous and widely published icons of the Mother of God. Poselyanin lists 16 variations of this icon celebrated on May 21, June 23 and August 26. The thin black line outlining the Mother of God indicates that the figures are painted on a dark background with a thin gold line outlining their robes. This sketch did not reproduce well, but there are several other beautiful designs for this icon elsewhere in these volumes.

3. **St. John the Forerunner**
    Св. Іоаннъ Предтеча
    Ст҃ы́й і҆ѡа́ннъ предте́ча

The Synaxis of St. John is on January 7. This sketch could be used to design an icon for a patron saint icon for a church or an individual. St. John's fur tunic usually is painted a blue-gray and his cloak may be green.

4. **Monastic Ss. Zosimas and Sabbatius**
    Свят. Пр. Зосима и Савватій
    Прⷣбный зоси́ма | прⷣбный савва́тїй

These saints are celebrated on September 27, April 17, and August 8. They are facing each other looking toward the inset icon of "The Sign of the Mother of God." St. Zosimas holds a scroll on which is written, Нє скорби́тє, бра́тїє, но посемꙋ̀ разꙋмѣ́йтє, а҆́щє оу҆го́дна сꙋ́ть прєдъ бг҃омъ дѣла̀ моѧ̀ бꙋ́дєтъ, то нє ѡ҆скꙋдѣ́єтъ ѡ҆би́тєль на́ша. "Do not be disturbed,

3

brothers, but understand the example in this way, if my deed will be pleasing before God, then our monastery will never be in want." The fine print beneath the feet of the saints says, "In the year 7194 (1686) - a painting by Simon Ushakov in the Solovki Monastery."

5. Jesus Christ "The Lord Almighty"
Господь Вседержитель
Їс хс гдь вседержитель

The Russian title given for many icons of our Lord Jesus Christ in these volumes is Спаситель "The Savior." Here, both the Russian title and the Slavonic inscription say, "The Lord Almighty." The inscription on the Gospel book is Прїидите ко мнѣ вси труждающїнса й ѡбременении, й азъ оупокою вы: возмите иго мое на себе й научитеса ѿ мене, іакw кротокъ есмь й смиренъ срцемъ: й ѡбрасщете покой дѹшамъ вашымъ: Иго бо мое блго, й брема мое легко естъ. "Come to Me, all you who labor and are heavy laden, and I will give you rest. Take My yoke upon you and learn from Me, for I am gentle and lowly in heart, and you will find rest for your souls. For My yoke is easy and My burden is light." (Matthew 11: 28-30 NKJ). This icon is also called "The Pantocrator."

6. The Monastic Saint Alexander of Svir
Св. Преп. Александръ Свирскїй
Стый прпбный алеѯандръ свирскїй

St. Alexander is celebrated on August 30. He is praying for his monastery to the Lord Jesus Christ.

7. The Holy Martyrs Blaise and Andrew Stratelates
Св. Муч. Власій и Андрей Стратилатъ
Стый сщеннмчнкъ власїй | стый мчнкъ андрей стратилатъ

The holy hieromartyr Blaise, bishop of Sebaste, is honored on February 11. The designs for his icons are used as models for many other saints in the literary patternbooks. St. Andrew is celebrated August 19. They are standing in prayer before the "Vladimir" Icon of the Mother of God.

8. Icon of the Mother of God "Of the Passion"
Страстная Ик. Богоматери
Ѡбразъ престыа бцы страстнїа

This is the Russian version of an original icon created by the Cretan painter Andreas Ricco as an artistic interpretation of the Greek liturgical poem: *(The Archangel Gabriel), who once announced joy to the All-Pure One, displays the future symbols of the Passion. Christ, however, incarnate as a mortal man, is frightened by the sight from fear of death.* The original icon was very wide spread in the 15th, 16th and 17th centuries in Italo-Byzantine painting and is now probably the most popular icon of the Theotokos among Greek Orthodox Christians. It is found in Russia in the 17th century. The "Passion" icon is really the "Hodegetria." It received the title "Passion" from the two angels who are depicted holding the instruments related to the Passion of our Lord Jesus Christ. On the top right the holy Archangel Gabriel is holding the lance and the reed with a sponge and on the top left St. Michael the Archangel is holding the Cross. Other versions add the crown of thorns, the nails, the container of vinegar, etc. (The verse cited above was often written in Latin or Greek under St. Gabriel on the Italo-Byzantine originals.) The "Passion" icon is celebrated on August 13. At least five of these icons were well-known in Russia at the turn of the century.

9.   St. John the Theologian
Св. Іоаннъ Богословъ
Ст҃ый їѡа́ннъ бг҃осло́въ

The Slavonic inscription says "St. John the Evangelist." The Gospel book is opened facing the viewer, въ нача́лѣ бѣ сло́во, и сло́во бѣ къ бг҃у, и бг҃ъ бѣ сло́во. "In the beginning was the Word, and the Word was with God, and the Word was God." (John 1:1 NKJ) The inscription in the ornamental frame says, и́же зато́ченъ бы́сть ѿ домети́ана царя̀ въ патмо́съ ѻ́стро́въ и та́мо ѹ҆вѣ́ри всѣ́хъ су́щихъ и па́ки прїи́де во є҆фе́съ. "Who was exiled by the Emperor Domitian [89 - 96] to the island of Patmos where he converted everyone there and returned again to Ephesus." St. John is commemorated on September 26, May 8 and June 30.

10.   The Image of the Mother of God "Bogolyubsky"
Обр. Б. М. Боголюбской
Ѻ́бразъ прест҃ы́а бц҃ы бг҃олюбскі́а

The title of the icon means "Beloved of God," the surname of the Russian Prince St. Andrew of Vladimir whose day is July 4. The most holy Mother of God is facing the Savior in the clouds holding a scroll on which is written, бж҃е, гд҃и, і҆и҃се хрт҃е, сн҃е мо́й, ѹ҆слы́ши моѐ моле́нїе. "Lord God, Jesus Christ, my Son, hear my prayer!" Kneeling before her in prayer is the monastic Saint Joseph, Hegumen of Volokalamsk, celebrated September 9 and February 13. He is identified by the Slavonic inscription: Пре́пбный і҆ѡ́сифъ волоколамскі́й. The "Bogolyubsky" icon is celebrated on June 18 and has many variations.

11. The Mother of God "Joy of All Who Sorrow"
Всемъ Скорбящимъ Радость Б. М.
Ѻбразъ прест҃ы́а бц҃ы – всѣхъ скорбѧ́щихъ ра́дость

This icon is celebrated on October 24 and has at least seventeen variations illustrating the good deeds which should be done by all Christians. The title of the icon is the first words of a popular hymn to the most holy Mother of God:"O Joy of all who suffer and Intercessor for those treated unjustly, Comfort for strangers, Haven of the storm-tossed, Healer of the infirm, Protection and Intercessor for the helpless, Staff for the aged: you are the most pure Mother of the Most High God: hasten, pray and save your servants!"[2] The inscriptions across the top read, left: Ра́дуйсѧ всѣмъ ра́дость. "Rejoice, Joy to All!" center: За всѣхъ мо́лишисѧ, блага́а, прибѣга́ющихъ съ вѣрою держа́вный тво́й покро́въ. "You pray for all those who hasten with faith to your powerful protection, O blessed one!" Right: Ра́дуйсѧ, блгⷣа́тнаа, гдⷭ҇ь съ тобо́ю. "Rejoice, full of grace, the Lord is with you!" The inscriptions on the scrolls held by Christ, the Theotokos and St. John at the top may be taken from icons described elsewhere. On both sides of the most pure Virgin's crown: Всѣмъ скорбѧ́|щимъ ра́дость. "Joy to all who sorrow." The scroll in the most pure Virgin's hand: Ѿ всепѣ́таа мт҃и, ро́ждшаа всѣхъ ст҃ыхъ. "O all-hymned mother, who bore (the Word,) holiest of all the saints."[3] In the box under her feet: На а́спіда и васілі́ска насту́пиши и попере́ши льва̀ и ѕмі́а. ҂а. "You will tread on the asp and the basilisk, and you will trample the lion and the serpent." [Psalm 90:13] The scrolls on the left side of the icon, from the top down: а́лчущихъ пита́тельница "Nourisher of the hungry." Стра́нныхъ оу҆тѣше́нїе. "A Comfort for strangers." Бо́льныхъ и҆сцѣле́нїе, немощы́хъ покро́въ и҆ засту́пница. "Healing of the infirm, protection and intercessor for the helpless." On the right: и҆ Ѻби́димыхъ засту́пнице. "And an Interceder for the those treated unjustly." Ѿбу́реваемыхъ приста́ннице. "A Haven for the stormed-tossed." Же́злъ ста́рости, ма́ти бг҃а вы́шнагѡ. "A Staff for the aged, the Mother of the God Most High."

---

[2] These verses were originally in the *"Prayer Canon to the Most Holy Theotokos, sung in every spiritual sorrow and difficulty. A Work of Theostiriktos the Monk."* Similar verses are found throughout the *Oktoich* and *Meneion*. See *Miraculous Icons of the Mother of God in Russian History*, page 114.

[3] These are the first words of Kondakion 13 of the "Akathist Hymn to our most holy Lady, the Theotokos." This is the Akathist sung on the Fifth Saturday of Great Lent. There is another "Akathist Hymn to our most holy Lady, the Theotokos, 'the Joy of All who Sorrow'" in the *Book of Akathists*, which appears to have been composed independently of these verses. The second Kontakion of the latter has the same content as *O Joy of all who suffer* but uses different vocabulary words in the original Slavonic.

12. The "Kazan" Icon of the Mother of God

Казанская Икона Б. М.

Ѻбразъ прест҃ыѧ бц҃ы казанскїѧ

The "Kazan" Mother of God is perhaps the most popular icon of the Theotokos among Russian Orthodox Christians. It is celebrated on Ocober 22 and July 8. Poselyanin gives 24 local variations of the icon. Perhaps the background of this icon was painted ocher. Then the letters of the inscriptions would be painted in gold on the red circle or lozenge.

13. Holy Trinity

Святая Троица

Ст҃аѧ трⷪца

This very beautiful drawing is faithful to the monastic St. Andrew Rublev's concept of the Holy Trinity. The palace, oak and mountain are very defined, and omitting the chalices to the right and left to the central chalice will make this design even more faithful to the Saint's design.

14. The Savior "Blessed Silence"

Спасъ благое молчаніе

Спа́съ благо́е молча́нїе

In the icon "Sophia - The Divine Wisdom" an angel takes God's rightful place of honor as the object of worship. (See the notes to Sketch 1:35.) In "The Savior 'Blessed Silence'" we see an angel with straight (as opposed to curly) hair dressed in the rank of angel called a "Virtue" representing the Holy Spirit. The angel is marked with the eight-pointed star of the Father designating the "Ancient of Days" and with the cross and the Sacred Name о Ѽн on the halo designating our Lord Jesus Christ (but without His initials і҃с х҃с), holding a key. Combining this symbolism we have an icon of the Holy Trinity. It is hard to understand the reason for naming this icon "The Savior." Our Lord Jesus Christ is certainly masculine. The Holy Trinity is also masculine.[4] Orthodox Christianity does not portray the Savior this way. This sketch is certainly an aberration and should not be painted or reproduced because it misrepresents our Lord Jesus Christ. Such an icon is certainly a source of bewilderment to ordinary people. The design could have been deleted from this book, but the details of the drawing (the hands, the miter, etc.) are very beautiful and can be used in the design of other icons.

---

[4] Those who are familiar with other languages know grammatically a **word** may be masculine, feminine or neuter. In Church Slavonic the words "Holy Trinity" are grammatically feminine but the Holy Trinity is grammatically masculine in the verbs. For example, see the morning prayer in any Church Slavonic prayerbook ѿ сна̀ воста́въ, "Having risen from sleep,. . ."

15. Miracle Workers of Yaroslavl

Ярославскіе Чудотворцы

Прп̑ный дѳ|о́дорх іа̑рославскїй

ст҃ый давı́дх | ст҃ый кѡнстантı́нх

These saints are celebrated on September 19. "The Monastic Saint Theodore of Yaroslavl" is the top inscription on both sides of "Christ Immanuel" and is in the center of the icon. St. David is on the left of the icon and St. Constantine is on the right.

16. The Holy Guardian Angel

Святый Ангелъ Хранитель

Ст҃ый а́ггл҃х хранı́тель

The Guardian angel is holding a scroll which says, ["He does not despise the stranger nor neglect the prayer of His poor man."] The quote appears to be a combination of two Psalm verses. The white feathers on the wings are represented by black.

17. The Monastic Saint Xenia

Св. Преподобная Ксенія

Прп̑бнал ѯе́нїа

The inscription says, "our mother monastic St. Xenia of Rome" who is celebrated on January 24. She holds a scroll on which is written Гд҃и їис҃е хр҃те́, свѣ́те істинны й ра́дость всѣ́мх, не пре́зрн призыва́ющихх та̀ ı́стиннѡ. "Lord Jesus Christ, Light of truth and joy of all, do not overlook those who call on You in truth!" Over her head is the "Holy Mandylion."

18. Fatherhood

Отечество

Тре́хх по́согла́сное бо́жество́у ѡ̑тцу́ й сы́ну́ й ст҃ый д҃у́хх

This is a representation of the Holy Trinity called the "Western Type." The icon showing God the Father with the Christ Child on His lap and the Holy Spirit as a dove is usually called "Fatherhood," often the Latin word *Paternitas* in popular literature. The grammar of the top inscription reprinted above is hard to decipher, perhaps: "The Triple Speaking-in-agreement Divinity: to the Father and to the Son and the Holy Spirit." The "Lord Almighty" is sitting to the left holding the Gospel open to Matthew 11: 28, the Cross in the center is marked "Jesus Christ," and the Father on the right holds a scroll on which is written а́зх е́смь сы́нх мо́й возлю́бленный "I am My beloved Son." Certainly this inscription must be a mistake because the Father and the Son are distinct Persons. The Holy Spirit is above in an eight-pointed star. They are surrounded by the symbols of the four evangelists: the man is not marked, the eagle is marked "Mark," the lion is marked "John," and the ox is marked "Luke." Variations of this icon were very popular and found almost everywhere. Over the centuries many western concepts were introduced into Russian iconography and were accepted as Orthodox. This icon has out-lived its usefulness as a representation of the Holy Trinity. Still worse the various Holy Trinity icons have become a serious hindrance to the conversion of Protestants to Holy Orthodoxy. Many Orthodox prefer Rublev's "Trinity" after they become familiar with it. As icons are replaced and church interiors are refurbished, the "Western Type" and "Fatherhood" icons should be replaced with the icon of the Holy Trinity in the appearance of the Three Angels, for example, see Sketch 1:13.

19. St. Simeon the God-bearer
Св. Симеонъ Богопріимецъ
Ст҃ый сѵмеѡнъ бгопрїимецъ

This theme is a detail taken from the icon for the feast of the Meeting of the Lord (*See Sketch 1:44 and the notes to this Sketch.*) The dark marks on the Christ Child's arms and legs are highlights.

20. Jesus Christ "The Lord Almighty"
21. The Mother of God
22. St. John the Forerunner

These three icons form a deisis group. The most holy Mother of God holds a scroll on which is written Влко мой, іисе хрте, сне бже мой, долготерпѣливый и многомлтивый. "My Master, Jesus Christ, my Son of God, long suffering and very merciful . . ." This text may be used elsewhere. The Savior is holding a closed Gospel book; Sketch 1:5 can be substituted where the Savior is holding an open Gospel if desired. St. John is pointing to a bowl containing the Christ Child which is a very graphic representation of the Most Holy Eucharist. He is holding a scroll Се, а́гнецъ бжїй, взе́млай грѣхи́ мира. "Behold! The Lamb of God who takes away the sin of the world!" (John 1:29 NKJ).

23. The Holy Forty Martyrs
Свят. Сорокъ Мучен.
Ст҃ін м҃ мч҃нцы въ е҃зерѣ

These holy martyrs are celebrated on March 9. Above them is our Lord Jesus Christ the Savior.

24. "The Unsleeping Eye of Our Lord Jesus Christ"
Недреманное Око Господа нашего Іисуса Христа
Недреманное О́ко гд҃а нашегѡ іи҃са хрт҃а

We see the Lord Jesus Christ as a youth resting on a couch with the Mother of God and two angels of the Lord attending Him. This is an illustration of Psalm 120:4 "He who keeps you will not slumber. Behold, He who keeps Israel shall neither slumber nor sleep." (NKJ). The icon is more decorative than devotional. An icon with the same name is a portrait of the Savior as a young man with His hand on His face, but His eyes are open.

25. Jesus Christ - "The Savior which is at the Savior's Gate in Moscow"
Спаситель что на Спасскихъ вратахъ въ Москвѣ
Ї҃с Х҃с г҃дь всєдєржи́тєль

The Savior is portrayed with the details of "The Lord Almighty" above. One of the gates with towers if the Kremlin in Moscow is still called "The Savior's" which formerly had an icon with a guard to make sure everyone passing by bowed and doffed his cap. The Savior is flanked by two angels of the Lord carrying instruments of the Passion. Kneeling before Him in prayer are the monastic Ss. Sergius [of Radonezh] and Barlaam [of Chutin].

26. The Seven Sleeping Youths in Ephesus
7-мь Отроковъ спящихъ иже во Ефесѣ
С҃тїи О́троцы, и́же во є҆фє́сѣ

The title at the top in Slavonic says, "The holy youths in Ephesus who slept for three hundred seventy-two years." The three saints at the top from left to right are і̑а́мвлі́хъ Jamblicius, ма́ѯїмїлїа́нъ Maximilian and дїони́сїй Dionysius. The four saints beneath are мартїнїа́нъ Martinian, кѡнстанті́нъ Constantine, а̑нтѡ́нїй Anthony and і̑ѡа́ннъ John. Jesus Christ is in a cloud above them. Their feast days are October 22 and August 4.

27. Jesus Christ "The Merciful Savior"
Спаситель Милостивый
Ї҃с Х҃с всєдєржи́тєль

This icon is similar to Sketch 1:25 but portrays an unspecified monastic St. Paisius с҃ты́й прпⷣбный паі́сїй.

28. St. Michael the Archangel
Св. Михаилъ Архангелъ
С҃ты́й мїхаи́лъ а҆рха́ггл҃ъ

This is a representation of St. Michael as a warrior with scarlet wings, cloak, short tunic and leggings. His crown, breastplate, Gospel book, trumpet, saddle and other details would be gold, richly adorned with pearls and jewels. He is holding a spear, a rainbow of many colors, a cross and a thurible. He is mounted on a scarlet winged horse over a burning city falling into an abyss. He is spearing what must be a demon with a face on its stomach. The cloud under his boot is blue as well as the cloud in which the Christ Child is standing behind a holy table with a cross and Gospel book. (Other icons show a hand blessing from heaven and a chalice and discos on the altar.) The overabundance of details that would distract the parishioners make this design unsuitable for icons that will be venerated in church on St. Michael's day, November 8.

29. Jesus Christ "The Lord Immanuel"
Господь Еммануилъ
Ї҃с х҃с г҃дь є҆ммануилъ

This is part of an "Angel Deisis" together with Sketches 1:30 and 1:31. According to Matthew 1:23 *Immanuel* means "God with us." The Christ Child usually has bright gold robes. See Sketch 1:73 for proper inscriptions.

30. St. Michael the Archangel
Св. Михаилъ Архангелъ
С҃тый мїхаилъ а҆рхаг҃глъ

31. St. Gabriel the Archangel
Св. Гавріилъ Архангелъ
С҃тый гавріилъ а҆рхаг҃глъ

The archangels are in prayer before Christ. The little bit that shows of their wings and robes are painted the usual way.

32. St. John the Forerunner
Св. Їоаннъ Предтеча
С҃тый і҆ѡаннъ пред҃теча

This is part of a deisis group with the Savior and the Theotokos which depicts only their heads, similar to the "Angel Deisis" in sketches 1:29, 1:30 and 1:31.

33. "The Entire Creation Rejoices In You, O Full of Grace"
О Тебѣ Радуется Обрадованная Всякая Тварь
Ѡ҆ тебѣ̀ ра́дуетсѧ ѻ҆бра́дованнаѧ всѧ́каѧ тва́рь

This icon illustrates the hymn to the Mother of God sometimes sung at the Liturgy of St. Basil the Great instead of "Worthy It Is." The sun со́лнце is marked in the upper left hand corner, and the moon лу́на on the right. Many saints are depicted, among whom are St. John of Damascus on the left holding a scroll with the opening words of this hymn which he composed[5], and on the right is St. John the Forerunner with his scroll. On the left under one of the trees one sees the word раи̇ which means "Paradise."

---

[5] *Oktoich* - The Book of the Eight Tones, Tone Eight, Sunday Matins, the Hymn to the Mother of God after the second reading from the Psalter

34. **"On the Throne"**

На Престолѣ бѣхъ со Отцем и Сыномъ и Св. Духомъ

Нл престолѣ бѣхх со Отцемх й сыномх й стымх дꙋхомх

The Slavonic and Russian titles say, "I was on the Throne together with the Father and with the Son and with the Holy Spirit." This drawing is similar to Sketch 1:18 "Fatherhood" or "Western Type" with the symbols of the four evangelist depicted on open royal doors. There are also seraphim and the Cross marked "Jesus Christ" on an altar with the Gospel book. The title is problematic because only the Cross could be the speaker "I," and the Cross is not a Person of the Holy Trinity. The Cross is the sacred sign of our salvation, but not God. Certainly, this design should not be reproduced or executed as an icon.

35. **Sophia The Divine Wisdom**

Софіа Премудрость Божія

Ѡбразх софін премꙋдростъ бжїн

This sketch is explained more fully in *An Iconographer's Notebook*.[6] The personification is attended by the most holy Mother of God holding a disc with the Lord "Immanuel" and St. John the Forerunner. They are standing on precious "cathedras" like bishops. Our Lord Jesus Christ is blessing over Sophia's head. Above are angels on both sides of the "Prepared Throne." Certainly this icon is uncanonical because an imaginary person has been placed on God's throne and receives the worship belonging to God Himself, our Lord Jesus Christ.

36. **Monastic Saint Paphnutius Borovski**

Св. Преп. Пафнутій Боровскій

Ст. преподобный пафнꙋтїн боровскый чꙋдотрорецх

This saint is commemorated on May 1. His scroll says, "Take heed for yourselves, brothers, before the fear of God and man."

37. **Holy Prophet Elias**

Св. Пророкъ Ілія

Ѡгненое восхожденїе пророка бжїа ілїн

The Slavonic inscription says, "The Fiery Ascent of the Prophet of God Elias." Below and to the right of the title field we see Elisha looking up to Elias, and again picking up the mantle which has fallen from heaven. To the left we see St. Elias, below he is being fed by an angel and again he is resting.

---

[6] Section 19, page 32.

38. Miracle Workers of Moscow

Московскіе Чудотворцы

Ѻ агіос а̀леѯій митрополітъ; пе́тръ митрополітъ;

і̇с χс; і̇ѡ́на митрополітъ; фі̇ли́ппъ митрополітъ

The Slavonic inscription says, "Saints Alexis, Metropolitan; Peter, Metropolitan; IC XC; Jonah, Metropolitan; Philip, Metropolitan." These saints are celebrated together on October 5. Although St. Philip of Moscow died in 1569, his commemoration was combined with the first three saints in 1875, effectively dating the icon to 1875 or later. Our Lord is represented on the Holy Mandylion supported by two angels.

39. Miracle Workers of Moscow

Московскіе Чудотворцы

Ст҃ый пе́тръ митрополітъ; ст҃а́а тр҃ца; ст҃ый і̇ѡ́на митрополітъ; | а̀леѯій митрополітъ;

The Slavonic inscription says, "St. Peter, Metropolitan" on the left, "Holy Trinity" in the center, St. Jonah, Metropolitan; St. Alexis, Metropolitan" center, below the Holy Trinity. These three saints have been celebrated together on October 5 since 1596.

40. The Mother of God "The Unburnt Bush"

Неопалимая Купина Б. М.

Ѻ́бразъ прест҃ы́а бц҃ы неѡпали́маа кꙋ́пина̀

This is an elaborate version of the holy prophet Moses' vision of the unburnt bush in the Old Testament. The inscriptions have not been preserved on this sketch. On an eight-pointed star we see the Mother of God with the Christ Child. She is holding the ladder from Jacob's dream and on her chest is Christ again as the Great High Priest on a rock from Daniel's vision. Around her are several seraphim in a circle. The upper four-pointed star has a number of angels. In the lower four-pointed star are the symbols of the four evangelists: the winged lion and ox, the angel and the eagle. In the heart-shaped fields between the eight points are angels holding various items symbolizing the Mother of God; the golden jar, etc. In the upper left hand corner we see the vision of Moses of the Sign of the Mother of God in the burning bush with an angel speaking. Notice his hand is raised in the orator's position. In the upper right hand corner an unidentified person is sleeping. [This field should depict the vision of the holy prophet Isaiah.] The lower left hand corner shows the vision the holy prophet Ezekiel had of the Lord. The lower right hand corner shows the holy forefather Jacob dreaming. Angels are depicted on a ladder leading up to the Lord. "The Unburnt Bush" icon is celebrated on September 4. This sketch is much more complicated than the illustration in Poselyanin's book.[7]

---

[7] *Mother of God*, page 565.

41. Ss. Florus and Laurus
Св. Флоръ и Лавръ

а̑гг҃лх г҃днь пор҃ꙋча́етх ста́до до ст҃омꙋ флѡ́рꙋ и́ ла́врꙋ

The Slavonic inscription says, "The Angel of the Lord Entrusts the Herd to Saint Florus and Laurus." These saints are commemorated on August 18. In the upper field St. Florus is on the top left; the angel of the Lord is in the center and St. Laurus is on the right. They are depicted again in the lower field herding livestock.

42. Jesus Christ "Do Not Weep for Me, Mother"
Не Рыдай Мене Мати

Не рыда́й менѐ мт҃и

This theme is based on the Irmos of the Ninth Ode of the canon at matins on Holy and Great Saturday. *Do not weep for Me, Mother, when you see your Son in the tomb, Whom you conceived without seed in the womb: because I will rise and be glorified, and as God I will lift up with glory incessantly those who glorify you with faith and love.* Our Lord Jesus Christ, having been taken down from the Cross, is shown standing in the tomb in front of the Cross marked і҃ н҃ ц҃ і҃ "Jesus of Nazareth King of the Jews." This is the Orthodox form of the western "*Pieta.*" This icon would be venerated during the Holy and Great Friday services if no winding sheet (плащаница or *epitaphios*) were available.

43. The Theophany
Богоявленіе Господне

Бг҃оавле́нї̈е г҃да нш҃гѡ і҃иса х҃рта̀

This is a simple depiction of the Baptism of our Lord Jesus Christ in the Jordan River celebrated on January 6. St. John the Forerunner is identified on the left, the Holy Spirit ст҃ый д҃ꙋхх in the center, and angels of the Lord on the right.

44. The Meeting of the Lord
Срѣтеніе Господне

Ср҃ѣтенї̈е г҃да на́шегѡ і҃иса х҃рта̀

This feast day, also known as "The Presentation of our Lord in the Temple," falls forty days after Christmas on February 2. This sketch is very elaborate and is probably a tracing from an icon of the Palekh School. At the top center we see the "Ancient of Days" seated on the clouds and blessing with both hands. In the upper left hand corner we have an angel approaching the Mother of God with the Christ Child "Hodegetria" in a palace that frames them. The center field is the representation of the event: St. Joseph the Betrothed is holding a cage with the doves and listening to St. Anna the Prophetess behind the most holy Mother of God. St. Simeon the God-bearer is holding the Christ Child. Behind them is a palace representing the Temple in Jerusalem with the Altar and two facing cherubim. In the lower left hand corner Simeon is translating the Hebrew Scripture into the Greek Septuagint, specifically the passage Isaiah 7:14. "Behold, a virgin shall be with child, and bear a Son, and they shall call His name Immanuel," which is translated "God with us" (Matthew 1:23 NKJ). In the right corner an angel is showing St. Simeon a vision of souls being both rising from and plunging into the abyss. "Behold, this Child is destined for the fall and rise of many in Israel" (Luke 2:34 NKJ).

45. "Only Begotten Son and Word of God"
Единородный Сине и Слово Божіе
Ѻ҆дннорѡ́дный сн҃е и҆ сло́ве бж҃їй

This icon is supposed to illustrate the dogmatic hymn sung at the Divine Liturgy to conclude the Second Antiphon. At the top middle field dividing the title of the icon, "O Only Begotten Son and Word of God," we see the Lord Sabaoth in a circle, with the Holy Spirit depicted as a dove in a circle and Jesus Christ "Immanuel" sitting on seraphim, holding the Gospel in His left hand and a sphere containing the head of an ox. On either side of this central group are two spheres. The one on the left appears to contain the head of a woman and two others. The sphere on the right shows a figure speaking to another kneeling. On both sides are palaces and two angels. The two middle angels are kneeling in prayer to the Holy Trinity before them. Two more angels are standing on tombs holding spheres with the word ст҃ъ - "holy." One is holding a thurible. Below them in the center is a depiction of "Do not weep for Me, Mother." The lower left and right fields are more difficult. An unnamed warrior saint is sitting leisurely holding a spear. (Some icons identify him specifically as our Lord Jesus Christ sitting on a cross.) An angel is about to strike someone lying on his back with his throat bared and arms crossed. A demon is driving some strange nude beings into the abyss. Opposite them a seraph with a sword is over a nude man on a demonic horse (notice the birds' feet instead of hooves) with a spear and a basket on his shoulder. The horseman is trampling a number of what appear to be corpses. Certainly this icon is much more difficult to understand than the hymn:

O Only-begotten Son and Word of God, being immortal and freely willing for our salvation to become flesh by the Holy Mother of God and ever-virgin Mary, without change becoming a man and even being crucified, O Christ our God, trampling death by death, being one of the Holy Trinity, glorified together with the Father and the Holy Spirit, save us!

46. The Entrance into Jerusalem
Входъ во Їерусалимъ Господа
Вхо́дъ во і҆е҆р́Ѹсали́мъ гд҃а нш҃гѡ і҆и҃са хр҃та̀

This is a typical and straightforward design for the Palm Sunday icon. This sketch varies from the norm because of the second palace on the left side.

15

47. "Praises of the Most Holy Theotokos"

Ик. Похвалы Пресвятыя Богородицы

Похвалы престы́я бц҃ы

This sketch is a more elaborate design for this theme; it has 24 prophets instead of the more usual nine or twelve. From top to bottom in the middle field of the icon we see Christ "Immanuel" and the most holy Mother of God on a throne surrounded by a floral garland. Barlaam is underneath. [On the left are the holy prophets Elisha, Elias, Malachias, Aggai, Zacharias, Isaiah, Moses, Ezekiel, Habakkuk, Samuel, Michah and David. On the right are Jonah, Nahum, Amos, Joel, Jeremiah, Jacob, Obadiah, Haggai, Daniel, Solomon, and Zephaniah.]

48. St. Nicholas the Miracle Worker

Св. Николай Чудотв.

Ст҃ый николай чꙋдотво́рецъ

St. Nicholas of Myra in Lycia is probably the most popular saint of all time. He is blessing with his right hand and holding the Gospel book in his left. He is standing between miniature representations of the most holy Mother of God and the Lord Jesus Christ. They appeared to him on several occasions; once while in jail for striking the heretic Arius at the First Ecumenical Council. They reinstated him with the emblems of his episcopal office, namely the omophorion and Gospel book. His cloak is in the form of a cross patterned phelonion is richly decorated with a floral motive on the lining. Note the other piece of cloth on his left hip opposite the *epigonation* on his right. St. Nicholas often serves as a model for icons of other saints. The inscriptions usually have St. Nicholas' name in the vocative case form Николае Нїко́лае instead of the nominative Николай Нїкола́й.

49. Martyr Boniface | Holy Martyr Longinus

Муч. Вонифатій | Агіос Логинъ Мучен.

Ст҃ый м҃чнкъ вонїфа́тїй | ст҃ый м҃чнкъ ло́ггінъ

The holy martyr Boniface is commemorated on December 19. The holy martyr Longinus is commemorated on October 16. The black areas on their clothes denote brightened areas.

50. Glorious Martyr Nikita | Martyr Artemius

Хвъ Никита Муч. | Мученикъ Артемій

Ст҃ый великом҃чнкъ нїкн́та | ст҃ый великом҃чнкъ а́ртемїй

St. Nikita is commemorated on September 15 and St. Artemius is celebrated on October 20.

51. Glorious Martyr Christopher | Martyr of Christ Theodore Tyro

Хвъ. Мучнкъ Христофоръ | Муч. Хръ. Ѳеодоръ Тиронъ

Ст҃ый мч҃нкх хрїстофо́рх | ст҃ый вєликомч҃нкх ѳео́дωрх ти́рωнх

Although the glorious great-martyr of Christ, St. Christopher would become one of Christianity's greatest saints, his parents were of the lineage of the "Canaanees" or "man-eaters." This epithet does not imply that they were from Canaan or that they were cannibals, or as some foolish authors have implied that they were part canine, but rather that they were pagans, who offered up humans as sacrifices to the pagan gods. Originally named "Reprebus," he lived during the reign of Emperor Decius (201-251 A.D.). Raised in a dark and perverse culture where wealth, luxury and power, as well as courage and physical strength, were the most desired attributes, Reprebus excelled in the acquisition of these qualities. He grew into another Hercules, a man of handsome appearance, and great strength and stature. He was greatly admired by many in this pagan world, especially by women whose admiration he greatly desired. After a series of visions directing him to Christianity, he discovered that his handsome looks were more a cross than a blessing, a cross that was too heavy for him to bear. Pagan women were constantly at his door and would not leave him in peace. He began to pray fervently and to fast with the hope that by doing so the Lord would lift this heavy burden from him, and would also grant him the Divine and Life-giving water of Christian Baptism. He awoke one morning to the appearance of an angel who told him to take courage for the Lord was with him and would grant him his requests in due time. This vision proved to be a true one for he found that his handsome face had been transformed and was now disfigured, and his beautiful voice had become garbled in tone. He was overjoyed at these changes, comforted in the knowledge that the Lord was with him, for He had finally answered his request in such an unexpected way. He felt confident that the Lord would somehow grant his second request also, that of holy Baptism. Those who had once praised and admired Reprebus for his looks now insulted him with slurs such as dog-face and dog-head, and did all they could to avoid him. Paying no attention to their meanness, Reprebus went about the town admonishing those who persecuted Christians. St. Babylas baptized Reprebus with the name of Christophorus, which means the Christ-bearer. In the West, St. Christopher is recognized as a patron of travelers, and an intercessor in times of disaster, famine and especially, of plague; the black death was said to have suddenly ceased in Spain on his feast day. In icons he is depicted carrying Christ upon his shoulder, or with a grotesque face. However, he should not be depicted with the head of a dog, which some iconographers have done. The Great-martyr Christopher is commemorated on May 9.[8] St. Theodore Tyro is commemorated on February 17.

52. Martyr of Christ Procopius | Glorious Martyr Demetrius
Муч. Хрꙗ. Прокопій | Муч. Хрꙗ. Димитрій
Сты́й великомч҃нкꙁ проко́пїй | сты́й великомч҃нкꙁ дими́трїй

The holy great martyr Procopius is celebrated on July 8 and the holy great martyr Demetrius is celebrated on October 26.

53. Monastic Saint Sergius
Св. Преподобный Сергій
Препⷣбный се́ргїй ра́донежскїй

St. Sergius of Radonezh is among the most venerated of Russian saints. He is the founder of the Holy Trinity Monastery in Sergeiev Posad near Moscow. In this sketch he is shown in prayer before the Three Angels in the upper left hand corner marked ст҃аꙗ тро́нца "Holy Trinity." In the center field St. Sergius is lying on a bed attended by angels. In the lower left hand corner is a scene depicting his passing which is commemorated on September 25. In the center is a depiction of the finding of the relics of St. Sergius commemorated on July 5.

54. St. John the Theologian
Св. Іоаннъ Богословъ
Сты́й іѡа́ннꙁ бгосло́вꙁ

In the center field from the top down: Jesus Christ "the Lord Almighty" blesses with both hands. Below Him is a frame containing the title of the icon "St. John the Theologian." Below this the saint is sitting on a richly decorated throne with an eagle. His Gospel book is open to John 1:1. There are four fields depicting the saint teaching a youth to paint icons. Unfortunately the text is illegible.

55. The Ascension of the Lord
Вознесеніе Господне
Вознесе́нїе гдⷭ҇а нашгѡ і҃иса хрⷭ҇та̀

This is not a simple icon of the Ascension. It is distinguished by the three fields made by two groups of six apostles and the Holy Mother of God with the two angels in the center.

---

[8] Translated from the Spanish by Timothy Nikolau. Condensed from *Orthodox Life*, Vol. 42, No. 3, May–June, 1992, page 9 and following.

The angels are pointing to the Lord's footprint in a stone which is still an object of devotion for pilgrims to the Holy Land. Above is a representation of the Holy Trinity.

56. Emperor Constantine and Empress Helen
Царь Константинъ и Царица Елена
Стїи велнкїн царен н равноаплн конетантїнх н єлена

No inscriptions have been preserved on this sketch. Ss. Constantine and Helen, who are commemorated on May 21, are shown praying before the "Vladimir" Icon of the Mother of God. The center field depicts the finding of the True Cross and the raising of a young woman from the dead which are celebrated on March 6.

57. John Chrysostom, Basil the Great
Gregory the Theologian, Monastic St. Eudokia
Іоаннъ Зл. Василій Вел. Григорій Бог. Пр. Евдокія
Стый іѡанна златоѵста | стый васілій велнкїн |
ї хї | стый грнгорїн бгословх | прпбнал євдокіа

St. John Chrysostom is commemorated on November 13 and January 27; St. Gregory the Theologian is commemorated on January 25; and St. Basil the Great on January 1. They are celebrated together on January 30. St. Eudokia is celebrated on March 1. They are here shown in prayer before our Lord Jesus Christ represented by the Mandylion.

58. St. John the Forerunner
Св. Їоаннъ Предтеча
Стый іѡанна предтеча

The Decapitation of St. John the Forerunner is on August 29. The saint is standing in a stoney desert with a tree with an axe in it. St. John is holding his head in a bowl and a scroll on which is written, Покайтеса, приближи бо ся цтвїе нбное. "Repent, for the kingdom of heaven is at hand!" (Matthew 3:2 NKJ) Jesus Christ "Immanuel" is over him.

59. St. Nicholas the Miracle Worker
Св. Николае Чудотв.
Стый николай чѵдотворецх

This is the usual depiction of St. Nicholas. The Savior and the Theotokos are depicted full length.

60. The Theophany
Богоявленіе Господне
Бг҃оѧвле́нїе гд҃а чш҃гѡ і҆н҃са хр҃та̀

This is a more elaborate depiction of the Baptism of our Lord Jesus Christ than Sketch 1:43. Except for the Holy Name ὁ ὤн the inscriptions have not been preserved. Here the "Ancient of Days" holding a sphere is sending the Holy Spirit down from heaven. Our Lord is wearing a loincloth and has His arms crossed. In the upper left hand corner we see Satan tempting Christ on a mountain, and a little lower the Lord is going to be baptized. In the upper right hand corner we see Satan tempting Christ to jump off the roof of the Temple. Below the Lord is conversing with angels.

61. St. John the Forerunner
Св. Їоаннъ Предотеча
Ст҃ый і҆ѡа́ннъ предте́ча

The title says "Holy Prophet John the Forerunner." Here the saint is standing among trees on a mountain. St. John is holding the Christ Child marked і҃с х҃с in a bowl, an angel's staff and a scroll with "Repent, etc." Matthew 3:2. Jesus Christ on the Mandylion divides the title.

62. The Martyrdom of the Holy Archdeacon Stephen
Убіеніе Св. Архідіак. Стефана
Оу҆бїе́нїе ст҃а́гѡ мч҃нка стефа́на а҆рхїдїа́кона каменїемъ

St. Stephen is commemorated on December 27. In the Acts of the Holy Apostles Stephen "said, 'Look! I see the heavens opened and the Son of Man standing at the right hand of God!' Then they cried out with a loud voice, stopped their ears, and ran at him with one accord; and they cast him out of the city and stoned him. And the witnesses laid down their clothes at the feet of a young man named Saul. And they stoned Stephen as he was calling on God and saying, 'Lord Jesus, receive my spirit.' Then he knelt down and cried out with a loud voice, "Lord, do not charge them with this sin.'" (Acts 7:56-59 NKJ) The drawing is correct but the lettering is reversed in the original.

63. St. Michael the Archangel
Св. Арх. Михаилъ
Ст҃ый а҆рха́гглъ мїхаи́лъ

This is a representation of St. Michael as a warrior. This design is one of several suitable for icons that will be venerated in church on St. Michael's day, November 8.

64. St. Michael the Archangel

Св. Архангелъ Михаилъ

Ст҃ый а҆рха́ггл҃я мі҆ха́и́ля

This sketch is similar to 1:28, but with a hand blessing from heaven. This design is not suitable for icons that will be venerated in church.

65. The "Vladimir" Icon of the Mother of God

Владимірская Икона Богоматери

О҆́бразя пре́ст҃ы́а бц҃ы влади́мі́рскі́а

This sketch did not reproduce well, but there are several other designs for this icon elsewhere in these volumes.

66. St. John the Theologian

Св. Іоаннъ Богословъ

Ст҃ый і҆ѡа́ння бг҃осло́вя

We see the Evangelist (symbolized by the eagle) dictating his Gospel to Про́хѡря Prochor in an very decorative landscape. The saint is looking up to the Hand of God blessing from the clouds in the sky.

67. The Protection of the Most Holy Theotokos

Покровъ Пресв. Богород.

Покро́вя пре́ст҃ы́а бц҃ы

This feast is celebrated on October 1. In the center field from top to bottom: Christ is blessing with both hands, two angels of the Lord are holding the omophorion or veil over the Mother of God. Ст҃ый рѡма́ня St. Roman the sweet singer is holding a scroll with the first words of the Kontakion of the feast Дѣ́а дне́сь "Today the Virgin stands in the church..." Actually St. Roman is not involved with the event of the Protection having lived in a different era some five hundred years before. He is portrayed on the icon of the Protection because he is celebrated on October 1 also. In the lower left field we see і҆ѡа́ння St. John the Forerunner. Behind him is the ли́кя а҆п҃толя the Choir of Apostles lead by the holy apostles Peter and Paul. Beneath them are the holy fool for Christ Andrew, his disciple, St. Epiphanius and a woman. In the right field we see the ли́кя ст҃и́телей the Choir of Hierarchs lead by St. Gregory the Theologian and St. John Chrysostom. Beneath them are the holy Emperor Leo the Wise, St. Tarasius and another bishop.

68. St. Alexis the Man of God
Св. Алексій Человѣкъ Божій
Ст҃ый алеѯій человѣкъ бж҃їй

St. Alexis is commemorated on March 17. His scroll says, а́зъ є҆́смь сы́нъ тво́й алеѯі́й. "I am your son Alexis."

69. Ss. Michael and Gabriel, Archangels;
Ss. Peter and Paul, Apostles
С. Арх. Михаилъ и Гавріилъ. Ап. Петръ и Павелъ
ст҃ый мїхаилъ а҆рха́гг҃лъ | ст҃ый гаврїилъ а҆рха́гг҃лъ
ст҃ый а҆п҃лъ пе́тръ | ст҃ый а҆п҃лъ па́ѵелъ

This is a deisis group without the Lord Jesus Christ. The Angels are holding disks with our Lord's initials і҃с х҃с.

70. The Washing of the Feet
Умовеніе Ногъ
Оу҆мове́нїе ногъ

This scene from the Mystical Supper is often on "Week" icons for the Thursday commemoration of the holy apostles.

71. St. Mary Magdalene
Св. Марія Магдалина
ст҃а́а марі́а магдали́на

St. Mary Magdalene is celebrated on the second Sunday after Pascha together with the other holy myrrhbearing women. She has her own day on July 22. She has a perfume jar in one hand and a white or gold cross in the other.

72. Jesus Christ "The Lord Immanuel"
Господь Еммануилъ
і҃с х҃с є҆мман҃уилъ

See the notes for Sketch 1:22. The lettering should be inserted as in Sketch 1:73.

73. Jesus Christ "The Lord Immanuel"
See the notes for Sketch 1:22. This icon has the correct inscriptions.

74. The Crucifixion

Паспятие Господне

Раслѧ́тїе гда нашгѡ інса хрта̀

The Slavonic inscription says, "The Crucifixion of our Lord Jesus Christ." The title board on the Cross says, ца́рь сла́вы "The King of Glory." The woman on the left is marked Марі́а Mary, іѡа́ннх John, and ло́ггінх Longinus.

75. The Nativity of Christ

Рождество Христово

Рождество̀ гда нашгѡ інса хрта̀

The Slavonic inscription says, "The Nativity of Our Lord Jesus Christ." The angels are marked, "angels of the Lord." The Magi are marked волсви. The midwife Solome is named баба соломі́а. A young shepherd is reassuring St. Joseph the Betrothed by telling him about the shepherds' experience with the angels. The black marks on the mountains are highlights.

76. St. Nicholas the Miracle Worker

Св. Николае Чудотв.

Сты́й николай чудотво́рецх

Here St. Nicholas has a very rich cross patterned phelonion. The black lines on the Gospel book are gold highlights.

77. St. Nicholas the Miracle Worker

Св. Николае Чудотв.

Сты́й николай чудотво́рецх

This is a very popular icon of St. Nicholas showing just his head and shoulders. It is not part of a deisis group.

78. St. George the Victorious

Св. Георгій Побѣдоносецъ

Сты́й великомчнкх гешргій

The Slavonic title says "Holy Great Martyr George." He is depicted as a beardless young man holding a sword and behind him are a shield and a quiver with arrows. Over his head is a very rich martyr's crown. St. George is a very popular saint and is celebrated on April 22. His icons serve as models for many other saints.

79. Jesus Christ "The Lord Almighty"

Господь Вседержитель

Їс Х̈с вседержи́тель

The notes to Sketch 1:5 may be applied to this design. Notice the Savor does not have a jeweled cuff. He does have a fold of His cloak on His right shoulder. The curls of His hair are on the opposite side.

80. Jesus Christ "The Savior"

Спаситель

This icon is similar to Sketches 1:25 and 1:27 without the angels. Here the Savior is blessing Благов́ѣрный кнѧ́зь мїхаи́лѧ тв́ѣрскїй чꙋдотво́рецꙗ the Orthodox Prince Michael of Tver whose day is November 22.

81. Ss. Boris and Gleb

Св. Бл. Кн. Борисъ и Глѣбъ

С̈т̈ый м̈ӵнкꙗ кнѧ́зꙗ бори́сꙗ | с̈т̈ый м̈ӵнкꙗ кнѧ́зꙗ глѣ́бꙗ

The Slavonic inscription says "The Holy Martyr Prince Boris | The Holy Martyr Prince Gleb." They are standing in prayer before "The Lord Immanuel." The saints are commemorated on July 24.

82. St. Demetrius the Crown Prince

Св. Димитрій Царевичь

С̈т̈ый благов́ѣрный цр́евичь дими́трїй

St. Demetrius of Moscow was eight years old when he was murdered in 1591. He is commemorated on May 15. The miniature scenes depict his martyrdom. Notice the bell ringer on the left side. The saint is standing in prayer before the Mother of God with the Christ Child.

83. St. John of the "Ladder"

Іоаннъ Списатель Лѣствицы

Пр̈бный і́ѡа́ннꙗ спиꙗ́тель лѣ́ствицы

The saint is standing in front of his monastery holding a scroll, "See, brothers, how narrow the path that leads to the expanse of paradise, and how wide the path to hell." The details of the drawing are typical.

84. The Entry into the Temple
Введеніе во Храмъ Б. М.
Ввєдєнїє въ цє́рквы прєст҃ы́ѧ бц҃ы

The Slavonic title says "The Entry into the Church of the Most Holy Theotokos" which is celebrated November 21. Current Church Slavonic church books use the words вхо́дъ во хра́мъ "Entry into the Temple." The Mother of God's parents іѡакі́мъ і а́нна Ss. Joachim and Anna, and the priest Захарі́й Zachariah are marked. Above an angel of the Lord is feeding the young Mother of God in the Temple. She lived as a strict ascetic and did not eat the food that was served there, but gave it the poor.

85. The Holy Life-Creating Trinity
Св. Животвор. Троица
Ѻ҆́бразъ прєст҃ы́ѧ трⷮцы ѻ҆ц҃а̀ и҆ сн҃а и҆ ст҃агѡ дх҃а

The Slavonic title says, "Image of the most Holy Trinity Father and Son and Holy Spirit." Similar to the "St. Sophia" icons, we see the most holy Mother of God and St. John the Forerunner standing in prayer. The holy Archangels Michael and Gabriel are above them. St. Sergius of Radonezh and Barlaam kneel in prayer. But instead a personification on the throne we see the Ancient of Days holding an orb with the Christ Child on His lap and the Holy Spirit as a dove in a circle. This is an example of the "Fatherhood" or *Paternitas* icon. This depiction of the Holy Trinity is not appropriate.

86. The Nine Holy Martyrs in Cyzicus
Св. Девять Мучениковъ иже въ Кизицѣ
Ѻ҆́бразъ ст҃ы́хъ дєвѧти́ мч҃нкъ и҆́же въ кѵзі́цѣ

The Holy Mandylion divides the title. These nine martyrs are commemorated on April 29. The four saints on top are Ма́гнъ Magnus, Ѳєодо́тъ Theodotus, Ѳаѵма́сїй Thaumasius, and Фїлимѡ́нъ Philimon. The five on the bottom are Рꙋ́фъ Rufus, Ѳєогні́дъ Theognes, А҆нтїпа́трєръ Antipater, Ѳєости́хъ Theostichus, and А҆ртє́ма Artemas.

87. The Guardian Angel of the Human Soul
Ангелъ Хранитель Души Человѣческой
Ст҃ы́й а҆́гг҃лъ храни́тєль

The following prayer is written on the top margin: *O Angel of Christ, my holy Guardian and protector of my soul and body, forgive me all my sins of today. Deliver me from all the wiles of the enemy, that I might not anger my God by any sin. Pray for me, sinful and unworthy servant, that thou mayest present me worthy of all kindness and mercy of the All-holy Trinity and of my Lord Jesus Christ, and of all the saints. Amen.*[9]

---

[9] *Prayer Book*, Holy Trinity Monastery, Jordanville, NY, 1960, page 51.

In a house a man is praying before the icon of Christ. Then he is shown sleeping on his bed. The guardian angel on the left is driving a demon away. The guardian angel on the right is writing his good deeds on a scroll. (A similar angel used to be depicted at the doors of churches writing down the names of the faithful entering. A second angel recorded the names of those leaving early.)

88. The Monastic Saint Nicon

Св. Препд. Никонъ

Ст҃ый преⷣбный нíкѡнⷯ

St. Nicon of Radonezh is celebrated on November 16.

89. Monastic Ss. Zosimas and Sabbatius

Свят. Пр. Зосима и Савватій

Преⷣбный зосíма | преⷣбный саввáтïй

These saints are celebrated on September 27, April 17, and August 8. They are standing within the walls of their monastery and facing each other looking toward the Lord "Immanuel" above the monastery church. On the left St. Zosimas holds a scroll on which is written, "Do not be disturbed, brothers, but understand the example in this way, if my deed will be pleasing before God, then our monastery will never be in want." On the right St. Sabbatius holds a scroll, сиⷱ глаголетⷲ [неⷱелыⷯ водвⷮ] "This you say [?]"

90. Holy Hieromartyr Blaise

СВѦЩЕННОМ⳾ЧЕННКⷮ ВЛАСÏЙ

Ст҃ый сⷰіенномⷱнкⷯ власïй

St. Blaise is honored on February 11. The designs for his icons are used as models for many other saints in the literary patternbooks. He is standing in an ornate frame holding the Gospel book with a towel. The Lord "Immanuel" is over his head. The dark areas represent highlights.

The Postnikov Collection Vol. 2

ANTIQUE ICONS IN THE COLLECTION OF A. M. POSTNIKOV

1. The All-seeing Eye of God
Всевидящее Око Божее
Вѣвида́щее Ѻ҆ко гда̀ нш҃его і҆н҃са хр҃та̀

The first sketch attempts to portray a spiritual concept rather than a sacred person or event. The inscription says, "The All-seeing Eye of our Lord Jesus Christ." The figure at the top is titled Гд҃ь са́ваѡ́ѳъ the "Lord of Sabaoth." He is blessing with both hands as a bishop and has an eight-pointed star inscribed in His halo which reminds us of the perfect eighth day of eternity. This representation of God is also called "The Ancient of Days." On His abdomen we find the Holy Spirit represented as a dove in a halo, an element taken from the Theophany icon. They are flanked by two cherubim who are facing each other. Clockwise we have an eagle holding a Gospel book and wearing a halo with the inscription Ма́ркъ "Mark" in front of him. Next is another cherub, marked Херу́вімъ "cherubim." Then a winged-ox marked Лу́ка "Luke," and another cherub. Next is a winged-lion marked І҆ѡа́ннъ "John," another cherub, and finally a winged-youth marked Мат̱ѳе́й "Matthew." This symbolic depiction of the four evangelists is found very often in Russian iconography. At the top center of the circle we see the All-Holy Mother of God with her hands raised in prayer. In her circle are three more cherubim. In the inner circle at the top we see two eyes and a nose, on the sides two more separated eyes, and at the bottom the end of a nose and a mouth. This configuration is the basis for the title of the icon. In the innermost circle surrounded by the eyes we have the Lord Jesus Christ "Immanuel." The original intent of the iconographer probably was to remind the viewer that we are all always in the sight of God. There is nothing hidden, secret or unknown to Him, but at the same time we are all also always in His care and protection as He is watching over us. Although the concept is edifying, the icon is confusing, typical of the complex didactic icons which were popular from the 15th to 18th centuries. We encounter a problem similar to the "personification" icons, such as "St. Sophia The Divine Wisdom." Here the eyes, nose, and mouth in the inner circle substitute parts of God's figurative or poetic "body" for the whole, which always results in something grotesque. For some reason God the Father and God the Holy Spirit are not represented in the innermost circle. We assume the original painter and his viewers were sincere Orthodox Christian who were influenced by ideas coming in from the west and considered this theme to be something pious. In our society there are many different forms of the so-called "New Age" pagan religion, among which is found also "The Cult of the All-seeing Eye" as explained in a book by the same name by R. K. Spenser.[10] This icon is not suitable for copying "as is," but the evangelist symbols arranged around the circle with cherubim, etc. might be useful as elements in another composition.

2.   Jesus Christ "The Lord Almighty"
Спаситель
Ïс χс вседержнтель

This volume is not onsistent with the first. The editors and call this icon "The Savior" in Russian. Sketches 2:2, 2:3, 2:4, 2:5, and 2:6 may be compared to sketches 1:5 and 1:79. Only in Sketch 1:5 does our Lord have His hair arranged on His left shoulder. This Sketch 2:2 has the Lord's cloak visible below His tunic's right sleeve. Notice the decorative gold stripe on the collar of the Lord's robe matching the clavus at His right shoulder.

3.   Jesus Christ "The Lord Almighty"
This sketch is a variation of the traditional pattern with gold ornaments on the Lord's tunic and different folds.

4.   Jesus Christ "The Lord Almighty"
Notice the different position of the Lord's left hand.

5.   Jesus Christ "The Lord Almighty"
This drawing varies the direction of the Lord's gaze. The black areas on the robe indicate highlights.

6.   Jesus Christ "The Lord Almighty"
This is a variation in the drawing of the cloak. The cloak covers one shoulder without the typical fold over the right shoulder held by the clavis. Note the ornamented cuff belonging to another tunic.

---

[10] Spencer, Robert Keith, "The Cult of the All-Seeing Eye," The Christian Book Club of America, P.O. Box 638, Hawthorn, CA 90250, 1964.

7. "Week"

Седмица

Ст҃ый їѡа́ннъ бгосло́въ | ст҃ый а́пла пе́тръ | і҃с х҃с | ст҃ый а́пла па́vелъ | ст҃ый нико́лай ч́ѹдотво́рецъ

The Russian word *sedmitsa* means "week." Usually "week" icons have icons of "The Resurrection" for Sunday, "The Synaxis of Bodyless Hosts" for Monday, "The Synaxis of St. John the Forerunner" for Tuesday, "The Annunciation" for Wednesday, "The Washing of the Apostles' Feet" for Thursday, "The Crucifixion" for Friday, and "All Saints" for Saturday; each icon representing the person or event given special veneration on each day of the week. A "deisis" icon portrays saints praying before Jesus Christ, the Lord Almighty. Therefore, this sketch is not a "week" icon but a "deisis" icon. Our Lord Jesus Christ is on His throne in the center as the "Lord Almighty" holding His Gospel book open to "Come to Me ..." Ст҃ый мїха́илъ а́рха́гг҃лъ St. Michael the Archangel and Ст҃ый гаврїи́лъ а́рха́гг҃лъ St. Gabriel the Archangel are closest to His head. Ст҃ый їѡа́ннъ пред́те́ча St. John the Forerunner is on the right and the most holy Mother of God is on the left. The Slavonic inscription at the top reprinted above reads, "St. John the Theologian, Holy Apostle Peter, Jesus Christ, Holy Apostle Paul, St. Nicholas the Miracle Worker." At the Lord's knees are a male saint and a female saint who may have been the patron saints of the couple who commisioned the icon. The inscriptions are illegible. At the Lords feets are Преп́бный зоси́ма | преп́бный савва́тїй the monastic Ss. Zosimas and Sabbatius.

8. The "Vladimir" Icon of the Mother of God

Владимірская Икона Богоматери

Ѻ́бразъ пре́ст́ыѧ бц҃ы влади́мїрскїѧ

Sketches 2:8, 2:9, 2:10, 2:11 and 2:12 are variations of the same icon as 1:2 and 1:65. In this sketch 2:8 the Christ Child's hand is in a different position. The fold of the Mother of God's cloak below her right hand is different.

9. The "Vladimir" Icon of the Mother of God

This sketch is not as tall and elegant as the ancient original icon.

10. The "Vladimir" Icon of the Mother of God

In this variation the Christ Child's face covers part of His mother's face. His left hand is in a different position. The Mother of God's head is bowed lower to the left than the ancient original.

11. The "Vladimir" Icon of the Mother of God

This variation copies the ornate gold crown that was added to adorn the ancient original icon. Here the Mother of God's head covering is ornamented and a separate garment from her cloak.

12. The "Vladimir" Icon of the Mother of God

This variation has the inscriptions in very ornate lozenges. The lozenge on the right contains the title ВЛАДИМІРСКАА "*Vladimirskaya.*" The sketch had the following inscription on the lower margin, "For blessed help this holy image was completed on June 16, 1716."

13. The "Vologodsky" Icon of the Mother of God
Вологодская Икона Б. М.
Ѡбразъ престы́а бцы вологодскіа

According to Poselyanin there are three miraculous icons of the Mother of God in Vologda: "Joy of All Who Sorrow," "The Sign," and "Kazan." These are all different icons. In this variation of the "Hodegetria" the Christ Child has an ornamental collar on His tunic.

14. The Mother of God "Joy of All Who Sorrow"
Всемъ Скорбящимъ Радость Б. М.
Ѡбразъ престы́а бцы всѣмъ скорбащимъ ра́дость

This variation does not have any inscriptions except the title and сонце "the sun." The center field has the "Fatherhood" image, below two angels with ceremonial fans are honoring the Mother of God with the Christ Child. The are seven scenes illustrating the hymn. On the left top, an angel is speaking and leading a group of people. Below this an angel is "clothing" the needy. A little to the right an angel is saving those on a ship. Below this an angel is feeding the hungry. In the center an angel is visiting those in prison. On the top right an angel is healing cripples. Below this an angel is healing the blind. A little to the last angel is leading prisoners out of captivity. On the bottom several prisoners are about to be executed, but an angel is comforting several others.

15. The Icon of the Mother of God "Of the Don"
Донская Икона Б. М.
Ѡбразъ престы́а бцы до́нскіа

The icon of Our Lady "Donskaya" appeared in 1382. The original icon accompanied the army of Prince Demetrius Ivanovich Donskoy to the Battle of Kulikolovo Field and afterwards was located in Kolomna near Moscow. Tsar Ivan IV Vasilevich had the icon translated to Moscow. During the siege of Moscow by Khazi Girey, Khan of the Crimean

Tartars, in 1591 Tsar Theodore Ivanovich had the icon displayed on the Sparrow Hills to protect the city. August 19 is dedicated to the remembrance of the saving of the city.

16. The Image of the Most Holy Theotokos "The Sign"
Образъ Пресвя. Богор. Знамение
Ѻбразъ прест҃ыѧ бц҃ы знаменїе

The Holy Mother of God holds her hands up in prayer. Jesus Christ "Immanuel" is represented on a disk on her chest. This is an icon of theology representing St. Mary carrying the Christ Child in her womb. The Savior is lifting His hand to bless. It is as if He were leaving heaven to establish an immediate contact with the viewer. There are some twenty-seven local varieties of this icon, most of which are celebrated on November 27.

17. Icon of the Mother of God "Life Bearing Fountain"
Икона Б. М. Живоносный Источникъ
Ѻбразъ прест҃ыѧ бц҃ы живоносный источникъ

This icon is celebrated on the Friday after Pascha. The design of the icon was unknown in Russia before the seventeen century. It was probably introduced from Greece to Russia by means of Mount Athos. The icon shows the Holy Mother of God in a fountain holding the Christ Child. They are flanked by the archangels Michael and Gabriel. Around the basin are the sick, crippled and blind taking water to drink or to wash themselves.[11]

18. The "Jerusalem" Icon of the Mother of God
Ïерусалимцкая Икона Б. М.
Ѻбразъ прест҃ыѧ бц҃ы їерꙋсалимскїѧ

This is a "Hodegetria" icon of the Mother of God which according to tradition appeared in the year 48 and in 413 was translated from Jerusalem to Constantinople.[12] The icon usually does not have the two angels in medallions nor the selected saints. This particular icon has the following saints clockwise around the margin starting at the lower left hand corner: Martyr Nestor, Martyr Carpus, Apostle Philip, Apostle Simon, Apostle Andrew, Apostle Luke, Apostle John, Apostle Peter, four Angels of the Lord before the Prepared Throne with a chalice, Apostle Paul, Apostle Matthew, Apostle James, Apostle Mark, Apostle Thomas, Apostle Bartholomew, Martyr George, and Martyr Demetrius. The drawings are all correct. The lettering for the Mother of God and the Christ Child was

---

[11] Skorobucha, p. 74.

[12] Skorobucha, p. 22.

traced correctly, but the lettering of the marginal icons was reversed. The feast days are on October 12 and November 13.

19. The "Kazan" Icon of the Mother of God
Казанская Икона Б. М.
Ѻбразъ прⷭ҇тыѧ бцⷣы казанскїѧ

This icon appeared in 1579. The Holy Mother of God appeared to a girl in the city of Kazan in a dream and indicated to her the place in which the icon was buried in the ground. After the icon was dug up in 1595 the Archbishop of Kazan assigned the feast day to July 8. At the order of Prince Pozharsky the icon accompanied the troops in the battle to free Moscow from the Poles in 1612. October 22 is the day of the freeing of Moscow ascribed to the intercession of the Holy Mother of God by means of her icon. In 1710 the icon was transferred to St. Petersburg by the decree of Tsar Peter the Great and placed in the St. Alexander Nevsky Lavra. The icon was placed in the Nativity of the Mother of God Church of Kazan Cathedral in St. Petersburg in1811. There are many varieties of this very popular icon. This sketch has Ст҃ый нїкифорх патрїархх the Holy Patriarch Nicephorus and Ст҃ый мⷱ архїдїаконх стефанх the Holy Martyr Archdeacon Stephen on the margins.

20. The "Kazan" Icon of the Mother of God
This sketch of the icon has a very fine expression on the faces with a double border on the Virgin's head-covering.

21. The "Kazan" Icon of the Mother of God
This sketch has a single border on the Virgin's head-covering. The clavis on the Christ Child's tunic has no ornament. The expressions on the faces are not as pleasing as Sketch 2:20.

22. The "Kazan" Icon of the Mother of God
Here the Mother of God has a crown and an ornamented head covering. Perhaps these details was painted to imitate the metallic crowns and jewels placed on especially revered icons.

23. Icon of the Mother of God "The Stone Not Cut By Hand"
Икона Б. М. Камень Нерукосѣчний
Ѻбразъ прⷭ҇тыѧ бцⷣы камень нерꙋкосѣчный

In the Book of Daniel 2:34 we read how the holy Prophet Daniel interpreted the king's dream. "You [King Nebuchadnezzar] watched while a stone was cut out without hands, which struck the image on its feet of iron and clay, and broke them in pieces." The "stone cut out without hands" represents both the Person of our Lord Jesus Christ and His Mystical Body, the Orthodox Christian Church. This is the kingdom of Jesus Christ which would be set up in the world in the time of the Roman empire on the ruins of Satan's kingdom. Among the kingdoms of the world The Orthodox Church is the "stone cut out of the mountain without hands" because it would be neither be established nor supported by human power or policy. No visible hand could act in establishing the Church, but it would be done invisibly by the Holy Spirit. The "Stone" or "Rock" is Jesus Christ, who was born of the Virgin Mary, the most holy Mother of God. In this icon we see the Mother of God with three women's faces in circles replacing the usual stars or crosses. Her morphorian is covered with meandering lines representing clouds are overshadowing a stylized mountain. On her breast is a circle with appears to be "Christ the King" or "God the Father" partially covering another circle with a crowned head perhaps representing the Holy Spirit. The Virgin's fingers are touching a circle with the words, "Rejoice, Gideon's Fleece!" The text on the lining of her robe is illegible.

24.   The "Kursk-Root" Icon of the Mother of God
Курская Икона Б. М.
Ѻбразъ прест҃ы́я бц҃ы кꙋрскыя коренна

This icon appeared in 1296 on the bank of the Tuskara River in Russia near the city of Kursk. The icon was found on the root of a tree, from which it has the distinguishing name "Of the Root." The icon "The Sign of the Mother of God" is in the center. The distinguishing feature of this icon is the detail that the Christ Child has both hands covered with His robe. At the top center is "The Lord Sabaoth" and clockwise the holy prophets Solomon, Daniel, Aaron, Elias, Habbakkuk, Jonah, Ezekiel, Moses, and David. Each is holding a scroll. Solomon's scroll says, "Wisdom has built herself a house;" Daniel's, "a Stone was cut out of a mountain without hands;" Aaron's, "The dry rod of Aaron was a sign of you because it bloomed without water;" Elias' scroll, "I have been very zealous for the Lord God of hosts;" Habbakkuk's, "You are the overshadowed mountain that I foresaw of old and announced;" Jonah's, "I called out to the Lord in my distress and He heard me;" Ezekiel's, "I called you 'the gate' and said, 'it will be shut, it will not be opened, and no one shall pass through;'" Moses' scroll, "I saw a burning bush not burning up;" and David's, "Listen, O daughter, consider and incline your ear." The icon is celebrated on September 8 and November 27.

25.   The "Virgin Before Birth" Icon of the Mother of God
Икона Б. М. Прежде Рождества Дѣва
✝ По рождествѣ паки дѣва ✝ прежде ржтва дѣва ✝ и в ржтвѣ дѣва ✝

The Mother of God and the Christ Child are enclosed in an oval surrounded by a decorative motive. The Slavonic title of the icon in an arch over their heads says, "* After giving birth again a Virgin * before giving birth a Virgin * and in giving birth a Virgin *." The Mother of God is wearing a crown and the Christ Child is holding an orb and scepter similar to the "Reigning" Mother of God icon. The text written beneath is the second part of a prayer that begins, "O, our beautiful mother! You are worthy of all good things, the enlivening and salvation of lost mortal men, accept this our unworthy prayer from your fallen and very sinful servants, in this time of bitter and tearful and sorrowful petition to you, for now joyfully with the angels we dare to say this prayer to you, the most holy lady queen Theotokos: [The text on the icon begins here:] "Mother of God, Virgin, Rejoice, Blessed Mary, for you have conceived the Son of God in the flesh! Rejoice, for you have carried Him in your womb! Rejoice, for you have given birth to Him! Rejoice for your breasts have nourished Him! Rejoice, for the Magi have bowed down to Him! Rejoice, for you have found Christ in the Temple! Rejoice, for Christ has risen from the dead and ascended into heaven! Rejoice, for you have been assumed into heaven! Rejoice, for you exceed the virginity of the angels and the glory of the saints! Rejoice, for you make peace on earth! Rejoice, for all the angels of heaven are subject to you! Rejoice, for whatever you wish you may request from your Son Christ our God! Rejoice, for you have been made worthy to be near the Holy Trinity! Rejoice, for you are the mother of the afflicted people who flee to you! Rejoice, for your joy will never end! Rejoice, O blessed one, the Lord is with you!"[13]

26. The Icon of the Mother of God "Growth of Reason"
Икона Б. М. Прибавленіе Ума
Ѻбразъ прест҃ы́а бц҃ы прибавлѣнїе оу́ма

This icon shows the Mother of God and the Christ Child. It looks as if their garments turn into a bell-shaped Russian-style priest's phelon. The text in the box underneath says, "A depiction of the most holy Mother of God with the growing into life to judge the living and the dead, protects from damaging winds, from damage from earthquakes, from attacks from wild and poisonous animals, from enemies and the revenge of blood feuds." Then, below, "March 23, 1734." Certainly the Lord Jesus Christ becomes flesh and blood Mysteriously by the priest at the Divine Liturgy just as He took flesh from the most holy Mother of God at the Annunciation. The attempt to depict the most holy Mother of God as a priest in this icon is certainly more confusing than edifying. Poselyanin does not list this icon in his index, so one would think it is not a canonical icon.

---

[13] *Christian Hymns*, page 12. [No author is given, but this prayer might be a composition of St. Dimitri of Rostov.]

27. The "Seven Lakes" Icon of the Mother of God

Седміезерская Икона Б. М.

Ѻбразъ прест҃ы́а бц҃ы седмїезерскаа

"The Seven Lakes" Icon of the Mother of God was enshrined in the Seven Lakes - Holy Theotokos Hermitage, a short distance from the city of Kazan. Seven small lakes surrounded the cloister, hence, the name "Seven Lakes." The hermitage was established by the pious monk, Euthymius, coming from a monastery near the city of Ustiug about 1615. He brought with him a wonder-working copy of the Smolensk Mother of God Icon as a blessing upon the new monastery. In the middle of the seventeenth century, when a plague spread throughout Russia, Kazan is reported to have lost nearly all of its 48,000 inhabitants. In 1654, the "Seven Lakes" Icon was glorified as a result of the protection from the plague given that city by the Mother of God. In 1771 another plague broke out and again the icon was brought to Kazan to save the people. To this day the icon is revered as miraculous as the faithful seek help from the Mother of God. The feast days commemorating the "Seven Lakes" Icon are October 13, June 26 and July 28.[14] This is variation of the Hodegetria type shows the Mother of God blessing instead of pointing with her right hand.

28. The "Smolensk" Icon of the Mother of God

Смоленская Икона Б. М.

Ѻбразъ Прест҃ы́а Бц҃ы Смоленскїа

The Hodegetria Icon of the Mother of God is very often found in Russian iconography aned is known as the "Smolensk" Icon. It is the classical representaion of the Mother of God pointing out the Way, namely Jesus Christ. There are many variations of this icon as seen in the following examples:

29. The "Smolensk" Icon of the Mother of God

The Christ Child is holding the top of His scroll.

30. The "Smolensk" Icon of the Mother of God

The Monastic St. Cyril is depicted in prayer before the Mother of God and the Christ Child.

31. The "Smolensk" Icon of the Mother of God

The Slavonic for "Hodegetria" is given here, Ѻдигитрїа *Odigitria*.

---

[14] Kovalchuk, page 94.

32. The "Smolensk" Icon of the Mother of God

In this variation the Christ Child's scroll is large and wrapped with decorative [red] ribbons.

33. The "Tykhvin" Icon of the Mother of God

Тихвинхкая Икона Б. М.

Ѻбразъ прест҃ы́а бц҃ы тѵ́хвинскїа [15]

This is a very widely published and popular icon of the Mother of God. The original appeared in 1383 over the water of the Tychvin River. The monastery that was established on the site was protected by the intercession of the Mother of God from the Swedes in 1613. The successful completion of the peace negotiations of Stobovo in 1617 were attributed to a copy of the icon. The Empress Elizabeth Petrovna and Tsar Paul I made a pilgrimage to this miracle working Icon. The feast day is celebrated on June 26.

34. The "Sweet Sorrow" Icon of the Mother of God

Образъ Пресв. Богор. Умиленіе

There are many icons of the Mother of God with the title "Sweet Sorrow." The name suggests the tender feeling in the representation rather than a type, such as "Hodegetria."

35. The "Sweet Sorrow" Icon of the Mother of God

This is another variation of the "Sweet Sorrow" icon. The Virgin's disproportionately small hand does not enhance the design of the icon.

36. The "Theodore" Icon of the Mother of God

Ѳеодоробская Икона Б. М.

Ѻбразъ прест҃ы́а бц҃ы ѳеодшршвскїа

The original is believed to be one of the icons painted by St. Luke the Evangelist. This one is named "Theodore," in Russian "Feodorovskaya," after the Church of St. Theodore Stratilates where it was located. The icon is celebrated on March 14 and August 16.[16]

37. The "Theodore" Icon of the Mother of God

This variation of the "Theodore' icon has simple square "stars" on the Virgin's robe and jeweled and decorated borders and cuffs.

---

[15] Тѵ́хфинскїа is also correct.

[16] Kovalchuk, page 34.

38. The "Theodore" Icon of the Mother of God

This variation is reversed; that is, it is a mirror image of the previous icons.

39. The Mother of God and Hieromartyr Blaise

Богоматерь и Священомуч. Власiй

ЙР ѲУ | ὁ ἅгίосх влаѣїй

The Mother of God is holding the Christ Child as a full length "Hodegetria" icon. They and St. Blaise are standing side by side. Icons of St. Blaise are used as patterns for many other saints.

40. Holy Prophet Elias

Св. Пророкъ Їлія

ἅгίосх пророка їлїта

In the lower right hand corner we see the angel speaking to Elias in a dream. His bottle of water is next to a tree. In the lower left hand corner the prophet is sitting in the cave being fed by the raven. Above the prophet is ascending to heaven in the fiery chariot assisted by an angel of the Lord. The holy prophet Elisha is receiving Elias' mantle.

41. Holy Prophet Elias

Св. Пророкъ Їлія

Ѿгненое восхожденїе пророка бжїа їлїн

"The Fiery Ascension of the Prophet of God Elias." This sketch is similar to the previous. The scenes are more carefully drawn and distinct.

42. Holy Prophet Elias

This sketch on the detail of St. Elias in the cave.

43. St. John the Forerunner

Св. Їоаннъ Предтеча

Сгый їѡаннх предтеча

This icon of St. John is part of a deisis group. The Saint is pointing to Jesus Christ as the "Lamb of God" on a liturgical plate. This representation the Holy Eucharist as the Christ Child is very common.[17] The scroll says, "Behold the lamb of God, who takes away the sins of the world. Repent, the kingdom of God is at hand!"

---

[17] See the notes to Sketch 2:93 "Behold the Lamb of God."

44. St. John the Forerunner

This sketch is a variation of the previous one. Notice that St. John does not have wings and the Christ Child has a scroll which says, [а́зъ є҆́смь хлѣ́бъ сше́дый съ нб҃се. "I am the bread that came down from heaven." John 6:41]

45. St. John the Forerunner

This sketch of St. John includes scenes from his life. Above is the icon of Christ "The Holy Face." The Saint is standing in the center holding a bowl with the Christ Child and a scroll. Behind him to the left we see his father, St. Zacharias, embracing his mother, St. Elizabeth. Under St. John's wing we see his birth in a palace. St. Elizabeth is assisted by several maids. To the right we see St. John baptizing people in the Jordan River. To the right and above we find the "Discovery of the Venerable Head of St. John" which is commemorated three times during the liturgical year.

46. The Twelve Apostles
Двѣнадцять Апостоловъ
Собо́ръ ст҃ы́хъ двꙋнаде́сати а҆пⷭлъ

The Apostles are holding a model of a church which includes an altar with the Precious Gifts prepared. Christ is blessing from above.

47. St. Nicholas the Miracle Worker
Св. Николай Чудотв.
ст҃ы́й нїкола́й чꙋдотво́рецъ

This is a classic iconographic portrait of St. Nicholas. The Slavonic inscription has misspelled "Of Myra in Lycia." Should be мѷрлѷкі́скый.

48. St. Nicholas the Miracle Worker

In the *Life of St. Nicholas* there are two occasions when Christ the Savior and the Mother of God appeared to the Saint. Once before he became a bishop and later when he was in prison for striking the heretic Arius.

49. St. Nicholas the Miracle Worker

The basic icon of St. Nicholas is very elaborate. The Savior and the Mother of God are depicted on thrones in heaven. The Saint's vestments and Gospel are adorned with icons. Notice the bishop's "Panagia" or "Encolpion."

50. St. Nicholas the Miracle Worker

This is a very straightforward design for an icon of St. Nicholas. Notice the unusual design of the ornament on the Gospel book.

51. Miracle Workers of Moscow
Московскіе Чудотворцы
о а̑гіос а̑леѯі́й мнтрополі́тъ; пе́тръ мнтрополі́тъ;
і҃с х҃с; і̑ѡ́на мнтрополі́тъ

Ss. Alexis, Peter, and Jonah, the metropolitans of Moscow, are standing holding Gospels with their left hands and and blessing with their rights. Their saccoses are very heavily ornamented. Notice St. Jonah's "bishop's cap" and the white cowls worn by Ss. Alexis and Peter.

52. Miracle Workers of Moscow
Московскіе Чудотворцы
о а̑гіос а̑леѯі́й мнтрополі́тъ; пе́тръ мнтрополі́тъ;
і҃с х҃с; і̑ѡ́на мнтрополі́тъ; фі́ліппъ мнтрополі́тъ

Ss. Alexis, Peter, Jonah, and Philip, the metropolitans of Moscow, are standing holding Gospels with their left hands and and blessing with their rights. Their saccos are very heavily ornamented. Notice St. Jonah's "bishop's cap" and the white cowls worn by Ss. Alexis and Peter. Above them is a marginal representation of a Deisis icon depicting the most holy Mother of God, the Lord Almighty and St. John the Forerunner.

53. Miracle Workers of Moscow
Московскіе Чудотворцы
о а̑гіос а̑леѯі́й мнтрополі́тъ; пе́тръ мнтрополі́тъ;
і҃с х҃с; і̑ѡ́на мнтрополі́тъ; фі́ліппъ мнтрополі́тъ

In this representation of the four metropolitans of Moscow the saints are all wearing bishops' caps that do not conform to the contures of their heads. The ornament on top makes the caps look more like modern miters. Our Lord Jesus Christ is represented as the Holy Mandylion.

54. The Holy Protomartyr and Archdeacon Stephen
Св. Первомуч. Архид. Стефанъ
С҃тый первомч҃никъ а̑рхідіа́конъ стефа́нъ

We see St. Stephen offering incense to the Savior blessing him from the heavenly sphere. Very often icons of deacon saints depict them with cloaks which appear as a pile of cloth on their left shoulders under the orarion. The elegant simplicity of this convincing design indicates the cloaks are are not necessary. St. Stephen is celebrated on December 27.

55. Holy Martyr Artemius
Св. Мыч. Артемій
Ст̃ый мч̃нкъ а҆ртє́мїн

There are several holy martyrs named Artemius. This is the miracle worker of Grom, Verkol and Pinezh in Russia. His feast days are June 25 and Ocober 20. He is dressed in a long Russian shirt and has a representation of the Lord "Immanuel" over his head. See Sketch 2:70 also.

56. Holy Martyr Boniface
Св. Муч. Бонифатій
Ст̃ый мꙋ́ч. вонифа́тїн

St. Boniface was a servant to a wealthy and dissolute woman, Aglae, in Rome, and had unclean and unlawful relations with her. They were both pagans. Aglae desired to have the relics of some martyr as an amulet against evil, so she sent Boniface to Asia to find and buy what she desired. Boniface took some slaves and money and said to Aglae: "If I can't find any martyrs and if they bring you back my body, martyred for Christ, will you receive it with honor?" Aglae laughed and so they parted. Coming to the city of Tarsus, Boniface saw many Christians undergoing torture. Boniface's heart was changed, and he repented of his sinful life with tears. He called out among the Christian martyrs: 'I too am a Christian!' The judge ordered that he be harshly flogged, that molten lead be poured into his mouth and, as this did him no harm, that he be beheaded. The slaves took his body back to Rome. An angel appeared to Aglae and said, "Take him who was at one time your servant, but is now our brother and fellow-servant; he is the guardian of your soul and the protector of your life." Aglae went to meet them, took Boniface's body, and built a church for his relics. She then repented, gave away all her goods to the poor and withdrew from the world, living a fifteen years in penitence. St. Boniface suffered in the year 290."[18]

"The Image, Life and Passion of the Holy Martyr Boniface" is the top inscription of our nine-paneled icon. Although the drawings are correct, all of the lettering was copied in reverse by mistake. It seems that iconographers were unaware that the Saint was a pagan until he saw Christians being martyred. The sketch is explained from left to right; top to bottom: 1. The inscription says, "Aglae calls Boniface and says to him, 'Now, brother, the time has come for you to bring the relics of the martyrs showing love.'" 2. The Lord Almighty is seated on His throne surrounded with cherubim and seraphim. Below we see St. Boniface crossing himself and opposite he is at the table with four others. The inscription says, "Boniface with joy is appearing prepared to complete the venture,

---

[18] *The Prologue from Ochrid* vol. 4, page 345.

taking gold he goes along the way with many others often diligently praying to God that he may hasten to complete the task for Him." 3. "And coming to Tarsus he sees many Christians by various tortures and being filled with zeal stands before the torturer confessing himself to be a Christian." 4. "And after many exhortations he was hung up upside down and suffering many tortures, calling on the Lord, he infuriated the torturer who ordered spikes to pierce his hands and feet." 5. "The Holy Martyr Boniface." The scroll says, "Lord, that they may be forgiven!" 6. "And seeing him unwilling to relent, the torturer ordered molten lead to be poured in his mouth but nothing hindered the Lord from helping the Saint" 7. "In the morning they tried other tortures and heating tar they put the saint in the vat." 8. "And seeing this the torturer fearing that he might suffer something worse himself, ordered his venerable head to be cut off with a sword." 9. "And his servants came and took his head, and recognizing and being amazed at his fortitude and thanking God gave the gold to the soldiers and took his holy body." The holy martyr Boniface is celebrated on December 19.

57. St. George the Victorious
Св. Муч. Георгій Побѣдоносецъ
Ст҃ый великомч҃нкъ геѡ́ргїй побѣ́доносецъ

St. George is probably best known for being the dragon slayer. This event is not recorded in his *Life* nor is it mentioned in the church service sung in his honor. This sketch corresponds more or less to the icon for November 26: "The consecration of the church of the holy great-martyr George which is in Kiev at the Golden Gate in 1037. St. George is in armor, with a scarlet cloak, a breastplate with a feather pattern colored ocher with white, a blue tunic, purple leggings, and sitting on a horse. The horse is white, the lance is poking the dragon, and behind him is a mountain, and before him is a city, before which a maiden is leading the dragon into the city, another maiden is opening the gates, on a tower is a middle aged king, and the queen, . . ."[19] An angel of the Lord is placing the crown of martyrdom on his head and the Lord's hand is blessing him from the heavenly sphere in the upper left hand corner.

58. St. George the Victorious and St. Demetrius of Thessalonica
Св. Муч. Георгій Побѣд. и Св. Димитрій Солъ.
Ст҃ый великомч҃нкъ геѡ́ргїй побѣ́доносецъ
Ст҃ый великомч҃нкъ димн́тїй мѵротóчецъ

Icons of Ss. George and Demetrius are frequently referred to as models for other saints. St. George is on the left and his curly hair distinguishes him from St. Demetrius who has

---

[19] *An Icon Painter's Notebook*, page 86.

a high forehead. St. Demetrius is usually referred to in the service books as "The Myrrh Flowing" because his relics exude a sweet-smelling liquid. This sketch does not have any inscriptions. The halos are indicated by circles of dots. The Lord "Immanuel" is in a circle of dots above them.

59.   St. Demetrius of Thessalonica
Св. Димитрій Солунский
Ї҃с х҃с | Ст҃ый м҃чнкꙁ димитїй солꙋнскїих побѣдоносецꙁ

This icon of an event in St. Demetrius' *Life* should not be confused with St. George slaying the dragon. They are very similar, but the details differ. We see St. Demetrius slaying Ц҃рь симаннна King Simyanin on horseback in an abyss. An angel of the Lord is placing the crown of martyrdom on the Saint's head while the Savior blesses from the heavenly sphere. Another angel of the Lord and two maidens are carrying an icon of the Saint. When we read the Service or Life of the Saint, there is no mention of the Saint killing anyone even though he was a military man. Rather, we find that while in prison St. Demetrius blessed the holy martyr Nestor (October 27) to fight and defeat a gladiator, the giant Lyaeus, in the arena.[20] [Perhaps iconographers needed an icon of St. Demetrius to correspond to St. George and they used a marginal scene from an icon of St. Demetrius which, in fact, was of St. Nestor.]

60.   Holy Martyr Menas
Св. Муч. Мина
Ст҃ый м҃чнкꙁ мина

There are two saints named Menas whose icons are very similar. This is probably the St. Menas together with Ss. Victor and Vincent celebrated on November 11. The lance in his hand is the distinguishing feature. The St. Menas with Ss. Eugraphus and Hermogenes on December 10 is holding a cross.[21]

61.   The Nine Holy Martyrs in Cyzicus and the Monastic St. Paisius
9ть Мучениковъ иже въ Кизицѣ и Преп. Паисій
Ѻбразꙁ ст҃ыхꙁ дѣвати м҃чнкꙁ иже вꙁ кꙋꙁїцѣ и прп҃бный паісїй

These nine martyrs are commemorated on April 29. Since there are no inscriptions, it is difficult to determine the identity of each saint. This sketch may be compared to Sketch 1:86. The details of the saints' beards, hair and garments do not match. St. Paisius is in

---

[20] *The Prologue from Ochrid*, Vol. 4, page 117.

[21] *An Iconpainter's Notebook*, pages 80 and 92.

the middle of the top row. There are at least four monastic saints named Paisius in the calendar.

62. Holy Martyr Thecla
Св. Муч. Ѳекла
Ст҃аѧ равноапⷭ҇льнаѧ ѳекла

The first woman martyr called "equal to the apostles" is portrayed in a charming landscape facing the most holy Mother of God holding the Christ Child in the heavenly sphere. She is holding one hand in prayer and a book in the other which is opened to "The heavenly God, the powerful God, the all-merciful God, whose heavenly kingdom will be for endless ages." St. Thecla is commemorated on September 24.

63. Monastic St. Alexander of Svir
Св. Преп. Александръ Свирскій
Ст҃ый прпⷣбный алеѯандръ свирскїй

St. Alexander is celebrated on August 30. He is holding a scroll which says, Не скорбите оубѡ братїа моѧ ѡ мнѣ но посемꙋ ѡбразꙋ разꙋмѣйте аще оугодна бꙋдꙋтъ дѣла моѧ предъ гдⷭ҇емъ, по ѡбитель моѧ не ѡскꙋдѣте но распространитсѧ. "Do not sorrow for me, my brothers, because I bear an image, you understand, which if my work is pleasing to God, my monastery will not suffer want but prosper."

64. Monastic St. Alexander of Svir
Св. Преп. Александръ Свирскій
Ст҃ый прпⷣбный алеѯандръ свирскїй чꙋдотворецъ

St. Alexander is called "the Miracle Worker" in this icon. He is holding a scroll which says the same thing as the preceding sketch. Over his head the Holy Trinity is represented as three angels, the center angel is identified as Jesus Christ.

65. Monastic St. Gerasimus
Св. Преп. Герасимъ
Прпⷣбный герасима йже на їорданѣ

The upper inscription divided by the Holy Mandylion says, "Arabic men fall on the donkey before St. Gerasimus' lion.[22] Image of the Monastic St. Gerasimus." The lettering was reversed in the original by mistake. The inscription of the central panel says, "Monastic St. Gerasimus of the Jordan." The panels are viewed from left to right, from top to bottom. 1. "St. Gerasimus pulls a thorn from the lion's paw." 2. "The lion leads the donkey." 3. "Arabic men fall on (i.e., steal) the donkey from St. Gerasimus' lion." 4.

---

[22] This inscription belongs to panel 3.

"Thieves steal the donkey while the lion is sleeping." 5. "St. Gerasimus feeds the lion bread and soup." 6. "Accused of killing the donkey, the lion humbly looks down." 7. "The lion, recognizing his donkey, tells St. Gerasimus." 8. "The lion brings the donkey and camels to St. Gerasimus." 9. "St. Izosimus comes to St. Gerasimus; the lion lies at his feet." 10. "St. Gerasimus blesses the lion to take leave from Gerasimus." 11. "The lion comes to Izosimus and not seeing St. Gerasimus, laments." 12. "St. Izosimus shows the lion the grave of St. Gerasimus; the lion lays down weeping on the grave and dies." St. Gerasimus is commemorated on March 4.

66. Monastic Ss. Sabbas, Stephen and Martyr Sabinus
Препод. Савва Стефанъ и Муч. Савинъ
Ст҃ый савва | ст҃ый стефанъ | ст҃ый савінъ

The monastic St. Sabbas the Sanctified (literally "the Ordained") is celebrated on December 5, St. Stephen the New Confessor on November 28, and the holy martyr Sabinus on March 16. St. Stephen is holding an icon of Our Lady of Vladimir.

67. Monastic Ss. Ephraim and Arcadius
Препод. Ефремъ и Аркадій
Ѡбразъ прпбнаго єфрема архімандрита
Ѡбразъ ученика єго прпбнаго аркадіа новоторжскаго

We see a very decorative border with the Lord Almighty at the top blessing with both hands. The inscription on the left says, "The image of Ephraim Archimandrite of Novotorzhsk" and on the right "The image of his disciple Arcadius." St. Ephraim is commemorated on January 28 and St. Arcadius on December 13.

68. Monastic St. Jerome the Desert Dweller
Препод. Їеронимъ Пустыникъ
Прпбный іеронумъ пустынникъ

St. Jerome is commemorated on the Saturday before Cheesefare Sunday, at Matins, Ode 9, tropar 2. The drawing is correct, but the inscriptions were reversed by the draftsman by mistake. Starting at the upper left hand corner, "When the priest remembers them at the Liturgy then they stand before the shining light." In the clouds we see souls holding their hands up to the light. Underneath them we see the monastic St. Simeon holding a scroll which says, "Remember, O Lord, [illegible.]" In the center at the top, "The Lord of Sabaoth." In the top left hand corner, "When they are remembered at the Panychida, they rest in the bosom of Abraham, Isaac and Jacob." Underneath in the clouds we see figures representing souls in the laps of Abraham, Isaac and Jacob. Beneath them we see a Bishop St. Sabbas holding a scroll that is illegible. Between them is the five-domed church of the Transfiguration of Christ. In the lower left hand corner we see God blowing on a man. A little above this is the inscription, "God created man in the image and likeness of Adam." In the lower right hand corner we see a woman reaching into a tree with a man behind her. The inscription above says, "The serpent led Eve astray and Eve led Adam astray." At the bottom center is a man wrapped like a mummy with his face showing. Beneath the inscription reads, "See me in the grave, the dead lying in the grave." In the main field of the icon is a man pointing to a crucifix above which is the inscription, "The monastic saint father desert-dweller and teacher of the Church." The Saint's name appears to have been omitted and the writing in the open book is illegible.

69. Miracle Workers of Novgorod
Новгородскіе Чудотворцы
Ѻбразъ новгорскихъ чꙋдотворцєвъ

At the top center is an icon of the Divine Wisdom over the inscription "Image of the Novgorodian Miracle Workers" in reverse. The names of the 68 saints are given as follows from left to right, from the top down:

Saints Artemius, Macarius;

James, John, Mstislav, Prince Theodore, Prince Mstislav, | James, Theodore, Cyril, Theodore, Cassian;

Glycerius, Longinus, John, Princess Anna, Prince Vladimir, | Cornelius, Acacius, Xenophont, Martyrius, Theophilus;

Isaacius, Dovmont, Nicephorus, Cyril, Nikita, | Ephraim, Sergius, Herman, Arsenius, Athanasius;

Nicholas, Theodore, Euphrosinus, Antonius, Nikodemus, Nicephorus, | Neil, Arsenius, Ephraim, Antonius, Antonius, Barlaam;

Sabbatius, Zosimas, Alexander, Sabbas, Melchizedek, Simeon, | Pimen, Martyrios, Alexander, Antonius, Gabriel, Alexander;

Luke, Basil, Gregory, Moses, Euthymius, Niphont, | Nikita, John, John, Serapion, Theoctist, and Joachim.

70. St. Artemius Verkolsky
Св. Артемій Веркольскій
Ст҃ый аρте́мій вєρко́слькїй

This is the same St. Artemius as Sketch 2:55. When the Saint was thirteen years old he went with his father into the fields where he was stuck by lightening and died on June 25, 1545. In 1577 a miraculous light shown over his grave, and his body was placed in the narthex of the church. From that time there were many miracles and a church service was composed to honor him also on October 20. This sketch shows the Saint in prayer before the icon Оу́спє́нїє ст҃ыѧ а́нны "Falling Asleep of St. Anna," the mother of the Mother of God celebrated on July 25.

71. Holy Princess Olga

Св. Княгиня Ольга

С҃тла книгина Ѻльга

Saint Olga is celebrated on July 11. The Slavonic inscription adds the word м҃ца "Martyr" by mistake.

72. Holy Princes Vladimir, Boris and Gleb

Св. Князья Владимиръ, Борицъ и Глѣбъ

С҃тый кназ борисъ | с҃тый кназ глѣбъ

С҃тый кназ владимиръ

St. Vladimir is honored on July 15; Ss. Boris and Gleb on July 24.

73. The Nativity of the Mother of God

Рождество Б. М.

Рождество престыа бцы

At the top we see the Lord of Sabaoth blessing with both hands. In the upper left hand corner the we see the high priest rejecting the offering of Ss. Joachim and Anna. A little to the right we see St. Joachim praying in the desert opposite St. Anna praying in her garden. To each an angel is announcing that they would be parents of the Holy Mother of God. In the upper right hand corner they are embracing at the eastern gate of the Temple. In the middle field to the left we see the usual depiction of the Birth of the Mother of God. A number of hand maids is waiting on St. Anna. To the right we see Ss. Joachim and Anna holding and rejoicing over the birth of Mary. In the lower left hand corner we see the maids bathing the infant Mary, in the center between Ss. Joachim and Anna, Mary is taking her first steps, and in the right hand corner Ss. Joachim and Anna are putting on a feast to celebrate the birth of Mary. The Church celebrates this feast on September 8.

74. The Nativity of the Mother of God

In this sketch some of the elements of the previous icon have been rearranged. From top to bottom, left to right we have the Lord Sabaoth, St. Joachim praying, Ss. Joachim and Anna embracing, a handmaid giving the child Mary to St. Anna, St. Anna praying, the birth of the Mother of God, maids bathing the child Mary and Ss. Joachim and Anna holding the child Mary.

75. The Annunciation of the Mother of God

Благовѣщеніе Б. М.

Благовѣщеніе прєстыѧ бцы

Above the Lord of Sabaoth is blessing. Below we see the Archangel Gabriel announcing to the Virgin Mary that she would be the Mother of God. More often icons show a dove representing the Holy Spirit descending from the heavenly sphere. This is the basic design for an icon of the Annunciation celebrated on March 25.

76. The Annunciation of the Mother of God

This is another sketch of the Annunciation icon depicting the Holy Spirit as a dove descending as a breath from the mouth of the God the Father in heaven. The Son is shown as a tiny figure in an almond-shaped aureole on the breast of the Mother of God.

77. The Annunciation of the Mother of God

This sketch is the basic design of the icon with realistic palaces.

78. The Annunciation of the Mother of God

This sketch shows God the Father giving His command to the Archangel Gabriel. Immediately below is the "Pre-annunciation" when Mary hears the voice of the angel while she is drawing water at the well. The icon shows St. Gabriel waiting for the moment when he makes his announcement.

79. The Nativity of Christ

Рождество Христово

Рождєство хртово

This is the basic icon of the Birth of our Lord Jesus Christ. At the top left is an angel, in the center is the star, and on the right and angel is announcing the Birth to a shepherd. In the middle to the left we see the wise men with their gifts before the Mother of God lying on a cushion; the Christ Child is in a tomb-like manger with the ox and the ass. Below a shepherd is telling the Righteous Joseph about the message of the angels and on the right the midwives are bathing the new-born Christ Child.

80. The Nativity of Christ

This sketch includes more of the Christmas story than the basic icon. On the top right the three wise men on horseback see the star being carried by an angel. On the left they are looking back. In the top center in a cave the angels are venerating the new-born Christ Child with the holy Mother of God; the midwives are bathing Him a little to the right. Below is St. Joseph with the shepherds and to the left an angel is announcing to the shepherds. To the right center, the wise men are presenting their gifts ; underneath an angel is speaking to St. Joseph in a dream. On the left is the flight into Egypt with Mary on the Christ Child on horseback accompanied by Righteous Joseph assisted by Joseph's son, James. In the center, a soldier is harassing St. Elizabeth with her infant son, St. John the Forerunner, but they escaped miraculously (see below). In the lower right hand corner, King Herod is consulting with the chief priests and scribes. In the center, the soldiers are slaughtering the children of Bethlehem, above the mothers are lamenting the deaths of their children. On the right St. Zacharias is being killed in front of the altar while a little above St. Elizabeth and St. John are hidden in a rock.

81. The Resurrection of Christ
Воскресеніе Христово
Воскресеніе хртово

The inscriptions have not been preserved on this sketch, which incorporates the Passion with the Resurrection of the Lord and following events of the Gospel. In the upper left hand corner we see the "Crucifixion of Christ," below this the "Descent from the Cross," a little below this the "Laying in the Tomb," immediately to the right the "Holy Myrrh-bearing Women at the Tomb," and above this the Risen Christ holding a banner appearing to St. Thomas and the Apostles in the upper room. In the top center we see the "Ascension of Christ," a little to the right and down the "Way to Emmaus" when Ss. Luke and Cleopas encountered the Risen Christ as a fellow traveler. In the lower right-hand corner the Lord is appearing to the Apostles at the Sea of Galilee and the scene above this may be a depiction of the Lord appearing to St. James, His stepbrother (see I Corinthians 15:7). In the very center we see a large image of Jesus Christ in an aureole rising from the dead, to the right are the soldiers "like dead men." To the left an angel is moving the stone and a number of angels are being sent down to the jaws of the abyss in the lower lefthand corner. The first angel is pulling a man by the hair, who may be the repentant or "good" thief who died on the cross with the Lord. A little left of center at the bottom we have the "Harrowing of Hades" with the Lord Jesus Christ pulling Adam and Eve out of the tomb, behind and around them are the righteous of the Old Testament. Many righteous have scrolls. Among the saints we see Abel wearing a skin coat. Although these saints are facing different directions, they are in a procession leading from the "Harrowing of Hades" between the soldiers and the "Appearance to St. James" to the gates of Paradise over which is a seraph. At the head of the procession is the Good Thief, followed by St. John the Forerunner, many righteous princes and king. Angels are meeting the procession. Behind the gates of Paradise we see the Good Thief entering into the "Bosom of Abraham." Abraham is in the center with many "souls" in his lap and accompanied by Isaac or Jacob. At the bottom next to Christ two angels are gathering sinners into the abyss. This sketch is similar to the following "Resurrection of Christ" icon.

82.   The Resurrection of Christ

This sketch is essentially the same as the preceding one. There are some addition details and the scenes are separated by mountains which make the icon easier to read. The inscription at the top says, "The Resurrection of Our Lord Jesus Christ" and is divided by the Holy Trinity showing the Father, the Son and the Holy Spirit with the Cross. The center shows Christ rising from the tomb, a little to the left St. Peter is in the tomb examining the grave clothes, the angel is announcing the Resurrection to the holy women, the Lord is sitting and speaking with the Apostles.

83.   The Creation of the World
Сотвореніе Міра

The inscriptions have not been preserved on this sketch, but the information has been correlated from Sketch 2:84. It seems the icons which attempt to illustrate biblical scenes and theological concepts are always much more difficult to understand than a Bible text or spiritual concept. Genesis has a reasonably clear description of God creating the universe and the holy fathers wrote sermons explaining everything. At the top field of the icon from left to right: first, we see angels around an aureole with the Crucified Savior on an altar being supported by what looks like a crowned woman with a halo seated on a throne and the Dove in a circle surrounded by seraphim. In the center is an eight-pointed star with God the Father resting on a bed, surrounded by angels and the most holy Mother of God "of the Sign" in concentric circles. A man, an eagle, a lion and an ox are in the corners of the star. God the Father is commissioning God the Son to the right. This connects the center circle to the right aureole where we see the Pre-Incarnate Christ also surrounded by angels. Below this are bands representing the heavenly spheres and faces in circles representing the sun and the moon. To the extreme right we see angels with spears driving the fallen angels down into the jaws in an abyss. To the left of the fallen angels we have a cycle of events from Genesis. To the far left we see an angel fashioning Eve from the sleeping Adam. Above this a nude figure is praying before a cross held by an angel. Inside the angel is talking to Adam and Eve; behind this they are before the tree of the Knowledge of God and evil. Behind this is the Gates of Paradise. behind this in a cave there they are lamenting the loss of Paradise. In a field outlined by a band an angel is speaking to Adam and Eve, below this Cain is stoning his brother Abel, in front of this Adam and Eve are lamenting the death of Abel. Surrounding this are angels blowing trumpets and inside the field are assorted animals.

84. The Creation of the World

Сотвореніе Міра

Господь савлодх сотворивый свѣтх ѿ небытіе во бытіе шестхюденми
вседмый же день почи ѿ всѣхх дѣлх своихх

The Slavonic inscription at the top says, "The Lord Sabaoth creating light from nothingness in the six days of creation but rested from all His works on the seventh day." On the left is an inscription "For our sake He deigned to become man" identifies Jesus Christ as a nude angel in an aureole surrounded by angels. At the center top is the "Lord Sabaoth" with the sun and the moon to His left and right. Below Him, Jesus Christ blessing with both hands. Below this is a number of spheres representing the nine ranks of angels. In the center circle God the Father resting on a bed, the Holy Spirit is a Dove in an eight-pointed star, and Our Lady "Of the Sign." An inscription says, "The Father says to the Son, 'My Son comes down to be similar to you.'" To the right of this is another aureole with the Lord Sabaoth holding the Crucified Lord which is surrounded by angels. The inscription says, "The Crucified Son resembles you." Returning to the left side of the icon under the first aureole we see an angel stabbing a demon with a spear. The inscription says "The Archangel Michael driving Satan out of heaven." Below this we see other demons falling into an abyss. An angel of the Lord is speaking to the demons falling into the abyss. The inscription says, "The Lord says, 'Driven out, humbled and condemned Satan to the abyss.'" In a depression in the top of the mountain left of center we see Adam and Eve; to the right Jesus Christ is speaking to them from the gates of paradise. Below them an angel of the Lord with an eight-pointed star in his halo is creating animals; below this the angel of the Lord is speaking. On the right side an angel of the Lord is speaking, in front of him an angel of the Lord is flying, below him an angel of the lord is dressed as a soldier. The inscription for the first angel says, "The Lord commanded Adam and Eve not to eat of this tree." Below this an angel of the Lord is speaking to Adam; the inscription says, "Adam names the animals." Below this an angel of the Lord is speaking to Adam and Eve, "The Lord blesses Adam and Eve and says, 'Increase and multiply yourselves and fill the earth.'" In the bottom center of the icon surrounded by angels blowing trumpets we see a man kneeling and holding his cheek. "After killing his bother Cain was grieved." Below this a demon is whispering into Cain's ear, who is holding a club and Abel is kneeling. To the right Adam and Eve lament Abel.

85. The Marriage Feast in Cana

Бракъ Въ Канѣ Галилейской

Бракх вх канѣ галілейстѣй

This icon in three levels is a straight forward depiction of the first miracle of our Lord Jesus Christ. The text is from the Gospel of St. John 2: 1-11. The inscription at the top center says, "There was a wedding in Cana of Galilee, and the mother of Jesus was there.

Now both Jesus and His disciples were invited to the wedding. And when they ran out of wine, the mother of Jesus said to Him, "They have no wine." Jesus said to her, "Woman, what does your concern have to do with Me? My hour has not yet come." The inscription on the left side top: "His mother said to the servants, 'Whatever He says to you, do it.' Now there were set there six waterpots of stone, according to the manner of purification of the Jews, containing twenty or thirty gallons apiece." In the right margin top: "Jesus said to them, 'Fill the waterpots with water.' And they filled them up to the brim. And He said to them, 'Draw some out now, and take it to the master of the feast.' And they took it. When the master of the feast had tasted the water that was made wine, and did not know where it came from (but the servants who had drawn the water knew.)" Left margin bottom: "The master of the feast called the bridegroom. And he said to him, 'Every man at the beginning sets out the good wine, and when the guests have well drunk, then the inferior. You have kept the good wine until now!'" Right margin bottom: "This beginning of signs Jesus did in Cana of Galilee, and manifested His glory; and His disciples believed in Him." (NKJ)

86. The Crucifixion with the Evangelists
Распятіе съ Евангелистами
Рас́па́тїе г҃да нш҃гⱳ іи҃са х҃рта

This icon may have been inspired by the traditional cover of a Gospel book used in church. In the center of an eight-pointed star we have a representation of the Crucifixion of our Lord Jesus Christ. and above the Holy Trinity in the appearance of the three angels. The four evangelists are in the corners. Top left is St. Matthew; top right, St. John; bottom left, St. Mark; and bottom right St. Luke.

87. The Appearance of the Mother of God Three Days after the Dormition
Явленіе Б. М. По Успеніи Въ Третій День
Ꙗвис́а ст҃а́а бц҃а по ou҆сн́єнїн своємꙋ в꙯ трєтїй дєнь ст҃ым꙯ апос́толом
христовым꙯ во трапєза

In monasteries there is a service called Чинꙋ ⱳ панагі́н "The All-holy" referring to the all-holy Mother of God. After Pentecost when the Apostles dispersed to preach the Gospel, they had a tradition, wherever they happened to be, at every meal to set a piece of bread set apart as Christ's share. When the meal was finished, they would say, "Glory to You, O our God, glory to You!" After the Apostles had been gathered together by the clouds for the Dormition of the most holy Mother of God, they were having a dinner on the third day after her burial. This time they added the words, "O most glorious miracle!" They saw the Mother of God, who had died, alive up in the air in a cloud surrounded by luminous angels. They said, "Most holy Mother of God, help us!" They returned to the grave, and not finding her body there, knew for sure they she had been resurrected three days later, like her Son, and had gone to heaven.[23] This icon is a combination of several independent icons. In the top center is the "The Divine Wisdom." On the left is the St. John representing the apostles holding the sun, the brightness of the Gospel and St. John the Forerunner, representing the prophets, is on the right holding the moon, the brightest light in the night of the Old Testament. They have crowns, wings and are busts of young men in the other. At the bottom center the Apostles are at the table seeing the vision of the Mother of God. The most holy Mother of God is in an eight-pointed star within an four-pointed star with the Savior above and the man, the eagle, the lion, the ox and seraphim. The holy prophets are on both sides, from left top to bottom: Moses, Zacharias, Ezekiel, Habakkuk, David, and on the right, top to bottom: Daniel, Joel, Zacharias [father of St. John the Forerunner], Solomon, and Jeremiah. The scrolls would be the same as the "Kursk-Root" icon on page 32. [Zacharias's scroll might say, "I saw the virgin as a seven-branched lampstand;" Joel's might say, "Your sons and daughters will prophesy;" Zacharias, the father of St. John, might say, "Blessed are your parents, O lady;" and Jeremiah's might say, "I saw you, O Israel, as a young maiden."

88. The Procession of the Venerable Wood of the Lord's Cross
Происхожденіе Чест. Древъ Креста Господня
Происхожде́нїє честна́гѡ и҆ животорѧ́щагѡ крⷭта҇ гдⷭ҇на

The Slavonic inscription says, "The Procession of the Venerable and Life-creating Cross of the Lord." More than five hundred years ago in Constantinople on August 1 there was a procession of the Cross from the domestic chapel of the Byzantine emperor to the great church of Hagia Sophia for the blessing of water. In this sketch for we see a four-cornered fountain, the Savior is in a cloud over the fountain, blessing. Bishops are standing on the both sides of the fountain, and behind them are priests and deacons. A king with a queen, princes and noblemen, old men, and young men are standing on both sides. Many men, women and children are behind the bishops on both sides. The most holy Mother of God is standing at the right side of the Savior and on the left hand is St. John the Forerunner. A narrow stream of water is flowing from the fountain which turns into a river. People are sitting, laying down, standing, crawling, and and all are suffering. They are drawing water from the stream and drinking it, and some are washing and getting well.

---

[23] *Large Prayerbook*, (in Slavonic,) page 153.

89. The Miracle of the Icon "The Sign of the Mother of God"

Чудо отъ Иконы Знаменія Б. М.

Чꙋдо ѿ іконы знаменїѧ бцⷣы

This icon represents a specific episode in the history of Novgorod. Prince Andrew Bogoyubsky of Suzhdal (1157-1175) wanted to subject the town on the Volkhov river to his growing power. A conflict between the two city-states broke out in 1169. According to tradition, the icon "Sign of the Virgin" was brought onto the walls of the town and was shot at by the Suzhdalians. She turned around to the town, shedding tears, which were collected by the archbishop on his omophorion. The Mother of God was honored in a similar way in Constantinople as the "Little Mother of the Town Wall" and protectress of the inhabitants. In this sketch the artist represented the events on the icon on three levels. On top we see Archbishop John coming out of the Church of the Savior holding a pole with the icon of the "Sign" and carrying it over the Volkhov bridge. The people venerate the miraculous icon before it is taken to the kremlin which the Suzhdalians are besieging. The attack by the Suzhdalians is shown in the level. They are shooting arrows at the icon, which is set up on the wall, but the Virgin turns away from the Suzhdalians shedding tears. The Novgorodians are seen at the bottom advancing the attack to avenge the affront to the Virgin. In doing so, they are supported by heaven. We see four saints riding at the head of the army: Ss. Alexander Nevsky, Boris, Gleb and George. In addition there is an angel striking at the Suzhdalians.[24]

90. The Vision of the Monastic St. Sergius

Видѣніе Преп. Сергия

Какѡ ꙗвиса стаѧ́ бцⷣа прпⷣбномꙋ сергїю

The Slavonic title says, "How the Mother of God appeared to the Monastic St. Sergius." In this sketch a scene is illustrated from the *Life* of St. Sergius of Radonezh (+ 1392) which is attributed to Epiphanius. According to the *Life*, the most holy Virgin, Ss. Peter and John the Theologian appeared to St. Sergius following Divine Liturgy. In the sketch St. Nikon is shown behind him. It is typical that the Holy Trinity be depicted at the top.[25]

91. "Let Everything that Has Breath Praise the Lord"

Всякое Дыханіе Да Хвалитъ Господа

Всѧ́кое дыхáнїе да хвáлитъ гдⷭа. Хвалúте гдⷭа съ нбⷭсъ, хвалúте его̀ въ вы́шнихъ.

This is an illustration of the Psalms 148, 149 and 150 sung at "The Praises" towards the end of the morning service according the liturgical usage. The inscription at the top says,

---

[24] Onasch, page 364.

[25] Onasch, page 382.

"Let everything that has breath praise the Lord! Praise the Lord from the heavens, praise Him in the highest!" Inside the margin line at the top, left and right, ᴀɴгєʌн ɴжє пρєʙышє ɴєʙєга "Angels which are above the heavens." The rainbow at top center: хʙᴀʌнтє єго ɴєʙєга ɴєʙєга "Heavens of heavens praise Him!" хʙᴀʌнтє єго голнцє н ʌᲈɴᴀ "Sun and moon praise Him!" хʙᴀʌнтє [єго] ʙга зʙ᪰зды н гʙ᪰тᲈ "All stars and light praise Him!" From around the central group of Christ the King surrounded by the nine ranks of angels and down among the representative creatures: птнцы пєρнᴀты, гɴ᪰гᲈ н ʙодᴀ, дᲈхᲈ ʙᲈρєɴᲈ, гρᴀдᲈ, н дρєʙᴀ пʌодоногɴïн, н ʙгн кєдρн, огɴь, гкотн, гоρᲈ, ʙгн зʙ᪰ρн, н ʙгн хоʌмн, гᴀдн, змïєʙн, ʙєздɴᴀ. Feathered birds, snow, water, storm wind, hail, and fruitbearing trees, and all cedars, fire, tame animals, mountains, all wild animals, and all hills, vermin, snakes and the abyss. In the banners over the heads of the groups on both sides, top to bottom, left to right: "Praise Him all angels!" "Praise Him all His angels!" "Sons of Israel [His] people!" "And all His Saints!" "Youths, virgins, the old with the young!" "Kings of the earth and all princes and judges!"

92. The Parable of the Rich Man and Lazarus
Притча О Богатомъ и Лазарѣ
Прнтчᴀ ѡ ʙогᴀтомᲈ н ʌᴀзᴀρємᲈ

This is a straight forward illustration of the Gospel text. The top inscription says, "From Luke chapter 16, reading section 83." In the center in the gazebo, "There was a certain rich man who was clothed in purple and fine linen and fared sumptuously every day." Underneath over the man on the carpet, "But there was a certain beggar named Lazarus, full of sores, who was laid at his gate, desiring to be fed with the crumbs which fell from the rich man's table. Moreover the dogs came and licked his sores." In the lower left hand corner, "So it was that the beggar died, and was carried by the angels to Abraham's bosom." In the top right hand corner over the cofin, "The rich man also died and was buried." On the right side in front of the demon with its hand raised, "And being in torments in Hades, he lifted up his eyes and saw Abraham afar off, and Lazarus in his bosom. Then he cried and said, 'Father Abraham, have mercy on me!' At the top left inscriptions "Holy Forefather Abraham" and "Holy Righteous Lazarus" The text continues, "But Abraham said, 'Son, remember that in your lifetime you received your good things, and likewise Lazarus evil things; but now he is comforted and you are tormented.'" (Luke 16:19-31 NKJ)

93. "Behold, the Lamb of God!"
Се Агнецъ Божій
Сє ᴀгɴєцᲈ ʙжïн

No inscriptions have been preserved on this sketch. We see the nude Christ Child lying in a chalice on an altar surrounded by two angels in a church with three domes. The text is words of St. John the Forerunner. This is a symbolic icon of the Holy Eucharist. Omitting the church building, the central design is very often painted over the top of the royal doors in churches in Russia.[26] Then the angels are each identified as "Angel of the Lord."

94. "Do Not Weep for Me, Mother"
Не Рыдай Мене Мати
Нє рыдай мєнє мати
On the left we see the Cross in front of the walls of Jerusalem, in the middle the most holy Mother of God, and on the right a curtain with the Slavonic inscription. At the bottom is a representation of Christ like those found on the "western style" shrouds still used in many Russian churches for the Holy and Great Friday services. The icon is unusual because it shows the hair of the most holy Mother of God.

95. "Do Not Weep for Me, Mother"
This icon is a variation on the Pieta and has the text of the liturgical hymn written around the margin.

96. "In You Rejoices"
О Тебѣ Радуется
Ѿ тєбѣ радуєтся шбрадованнаа всакаа тварь
This is a "week icon," a composite icon made up of icons of воскрєсєнїє хртово "The Resurrection of Christ," соборх архїстратига мїхаил "The Synaxis of the Archangel Michael," оусѣкновєнїє главы іѡанна прєдтєчы "The Beheading of St. John the Forerunner," Благовѣщєнїє прєстыя бцы "The Annunciation," оумовєнїє ногх "The Washing of the [Apostles'] Feet," распатїє хртово "The Crucifixion of Christ," and the central panel "In You Rejoices." At the top center below the main inscription is another within the border, Йже прєждє вѣкх бгх нашх "Who before the ages being our God." The New Testament Holy Trinity is in a four-pointed star with the symbols of the evangelists and flanked by the heavenly hosts. Beneath is a church шсвящєнный храмє "O consecrated temple!" архангєлскїй соборх "The Assembly of Archangels" surrounds the most holy Mother of God on a throne with the Christ Child. The text of the prayer is in the circle surrounding them. Below them, "St. John the Forerunner" и чєловѣчєскїй родх "And the human race." On both sides of St. John are с. п. іоаннх дам. St. John Damascene and с. п. Козма St. Cosmas holding scrolls. Beneath them the л. младєнцєвх "the choir of children." On the right side under the "Crucifixion" are the разбойникх "The Good Thief," дѣвствєннаа

---

[26] See Timchenko, pages 8, 14, 17, 22-23, and 65, for example.

"Virginal (with "Praise!" opposite)," лйлх постникх "the choir of ascetics," лйкх мȣченникшвх "the choir of martyrs," and лйкх апост. "the choir of apostles." On the left side beneath the "Washing of the Feet" are преп. Єѵросинїа the monastic St. Euphrosynia, похвало "Praise!" Then лйкх царнцх "the choir of queens," лйкх с. женх "choir of holy women," л. свАтителей "the choir of bishops," л. преп. "choir of monastic saints," and л. пророк "the choir of prophets." The current text of the prayer is, "All creation, the angelic assembly, and the human race rejoice in you, O blessed one, O consecrated temple, O spiritual paradise, O virginal praise, from whom our God, Who existed before creation, became incarnate and was a small child: for He has made your lap a throne and your womb wider than the sky. All creation rejoices in you: O blessed one, glory to you!"

97. "Our Father"
Отче Нашъ
Ѻбразх Ѻтче нашх йже єсй на небесѣхх, да свАтйтсА ймА твоѐ:

"The Image 'Our Father, who art in heaven, hallowed be Thy name'" is supposed to be a "mystical" icon, but the large number of figures and confusing details do not lead one to prayerful contemplation. The icon is didactic in its attempt to present a rational depiction of the Lord's Prayer. Unfortunately the result is more grandiose than edifying. Perhaps the design was influenced by western prints. The subjects and the correct order of the nine drawings are not obvious. Considering the icon from left to right, top to bottom: 1. "Thy kingdom come." 2. The representation of the Holy Trinity corresponds to "Our Father, Who art in heaven." 3. "Hallowed be Thy name." 4. "On earth as it is in heaven." 5. "Give us this day our daily bread." Christ is teaching the Apostles and behind them the Divine Liturgy is being served in a church. 6. Our Lord carrying the Cross illustrates "Thy will be done on earth as it is in heaven." 7. "And lead us not into temptation." 8. "For Thine is the kingdom and the power and the glory" is similar to the "Procession of the Cross" icon for August 1. 9. "But deliver us from the evil one."

98. The Liturgy
Литургїа
Лїтȣргїа

The title of the icon is inscribed in the box around the Cross at the top center of the composition: Закло превѣчнаго младенца гда бга и спса ншего нса хрта єже єсть агнецх бжїй "The Dividing of the Pre-eternal Child, our Lord God and Savior Jesus Christ, Who is the Lamb of God." Below this, гдь саваѡдъ, the "Lord Of Sabaoth." In the center we see an angel putting the Christ Child in a chalice. Behind him is St. Gregory the Theologian; to the right another angel and St. John Chrysostom, and behind him St. Basil the Great. On the left side we see an angel giving Holy Communion. This is written on the doorway, гдна врата | гдне праведный | гдне "The Lord's Gates, the Lord's righteousness, the Lord's [omitted?]" The following text is written around the margin: "A story by St. Gregory the Theologian[27] about the Divine Liturgy: Father sings the prokimen, but St. Michael says, "Wisdom!" And St. Gabriel, "Attention!" And Christ Himself, "Peace be to all!" Then all the faithful stand with fear in the Church of God, just like in heaven. They stand attentively. No one speaks about worldly things to his friends. They do not think about vain things. When they begin to sing "Alleluia," then the Son of God descends from heaven to be divided and to give Himself to all as food for salvation. When he [Father] begins to read the Gospel, then the Lord Himself teaches us for salvation. Brethren, stand with fear! Let no one speak about the vain things of this world, but rather with great love dispel evil memories. And when the priest says, "Let all catechumens depart," then one can see a demon standing before the church doors sticking out his tongue like an arrow of fire and gnashing his teeth against the man who fears God. But the Angel of the Lord protects him. And when they begin to sing the Cherubic Hymn, then all stand with fear and, looking down, pray with tears to God. And when the procession begins, then all the powers of heaven serve invisibly, not being able to gaze upon the mighty King of All being carried in. And when the priest says "Attention" then the angel of the Lord opens [His] side His blood and stands in judgment and cutting up His body and placing [It] on the paten. And It is truly the Body of Christ given to the faithful as food.*" This text is inserted in the left margin: Тѣло хрⷭ҇тово прїимѝте, і исто́чникѧ безсме́ртнаго вкꙋси́те аллилꙋі́ѧ: "Receive the Body of Christ and taste the Source of immortality: Alleluia!"

---

[27] That is, attributed to him. See "Anthology" in *An Icon Painter's Notebook*, page 2.

Tracings of Antique Icons in the Collection of A. M. Postnikov, 1898

This modest work is dedicated to
Professor Alfred Alexandrovich Parland
as a token of deep respect and sincere dedication.
The Author - V. I. Uspensky

LIST OF SKETCHES

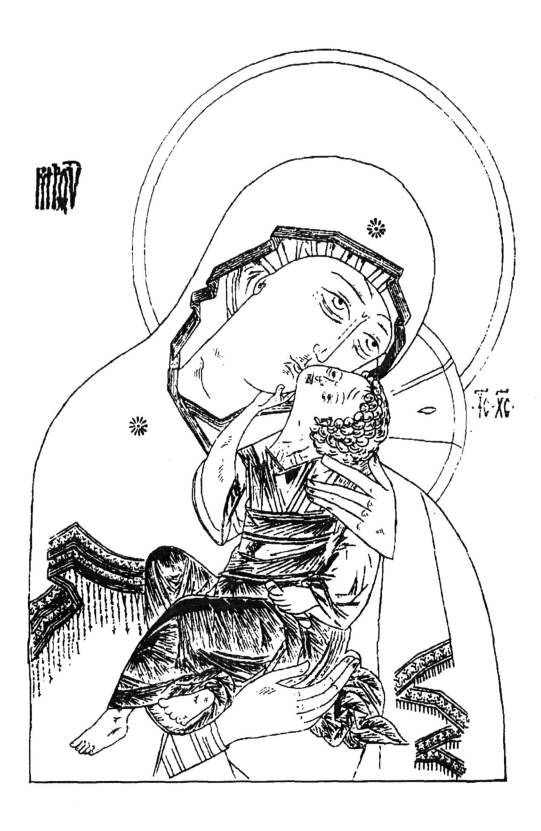

Sketch 1. Most Holy Mother of God "Sweet Sorrow"

Sketch 2. The "Vladimir" Icon of the Mother of God

Sketch 3. St. John the Forerunner

Sketch 4. Monastic Saints Zosimas and Sabbatius

Sketch 5. Jesus Christ "The Lord Almighty"

Sketch 6. The Monastic Saint Alexander of Svir

Sketch 7. Holy Martyrs Blaise and Andrew Stratelates

Sketch 8. Icon of the Mother of God "Of The Passion"

Sketch 9. St. John the Theologian

Sketch 10. Image of the Mother of God "Bogolyubsky"

Sketch 11. The Mother of God "Joy Of All Who Sorrow"

Sketch 12. The "Kazan" Icon of the Mother of God

Sketch 13. The Holy Trinity

Sketch 14. Jesus Christ - The Savior "Blessed Silence"

Sketch 15. Miracle Workers of Yaroslavl

Sketch 16. The Holy Guardian Angel

Sketch 17. Monastic Saint Xenia

Sketch 18. Fatherhood

Sketch 19. St. Simeon the God-Receiver

Sketch 20. Jesus Christ "The Lord Almighty"

Sketch 21. The Mother of God

Sketch 22. St. John the Forerunner

Plate 23. Forty Holy Martyrs

Sketch 24. Jesus Christ "The Unsleeping Eye of Our Lord"

Sketch 25. Jesus Christ - The Savior which is at the Savior's Gate in Moscow

Sketch 26. The Seven Sleeping Youths in Ephesus

Sketch 27. Jesus Christ "The Merciful Savior"

Sketch 28. St. Michael the Archangel

Sketch 29. Jesus Christ "The Lord Immanuel"

Sketch 30. St. Michael the Archangel

Sketch 31. St. Gabriel the Archangel

Sketch 32. St. John the Forerunner

Sketch 33. "The Entire Creation Rejoices in You, Full of Grace!"

Sketch 34. On the Throne

Sketch 35. Sophia - The Divine Wisdom

Sketch 36. Monastic Saint Paphnutius of Borovsk

Sketch 37. Holy Prophet Elias

Sketch 38. Miracle Workers of Moscow

Sketch 39. Miracle Workers of Moscow

Sketch 40. The Mother of God "The Unburnt Bush"

Sketch 41. Ss. Florus and Laurus

Sketch 42. Jesus Christ "Do Not Weep for Me, Mother"

Sketch 43. The Theophany

Sketch 44. The Meeting of the Lord

Sketch 45. "Only Begotten Son and Word of God"

Sketch 46. The Entrance into Jerusalem

Sketch 47. "Praises of the Most Holy Theotokos"

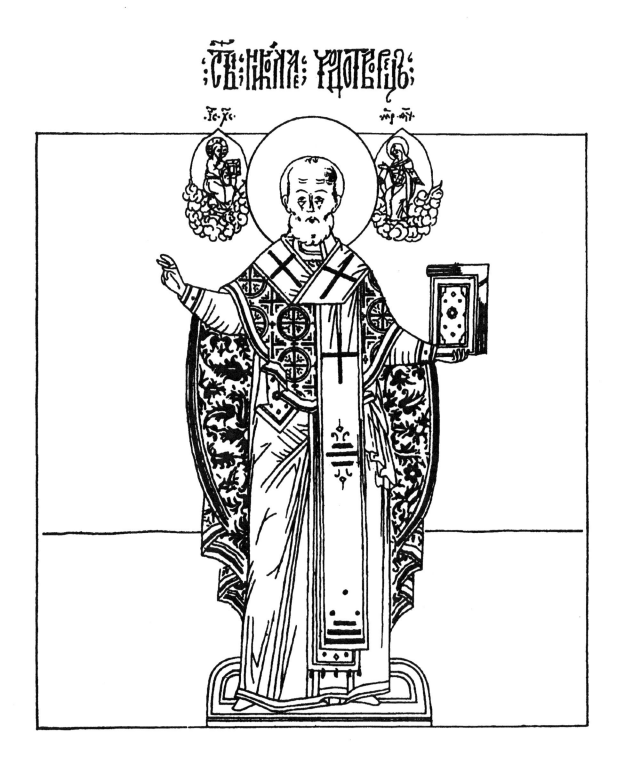

Sketch 48. St. Nicholas the Miracle Worker

Sketch 49. Martyr Boniface | Holy Martyr Longinus

Sketch 50. Glorious Martyr Nikita | Martyr Artemius

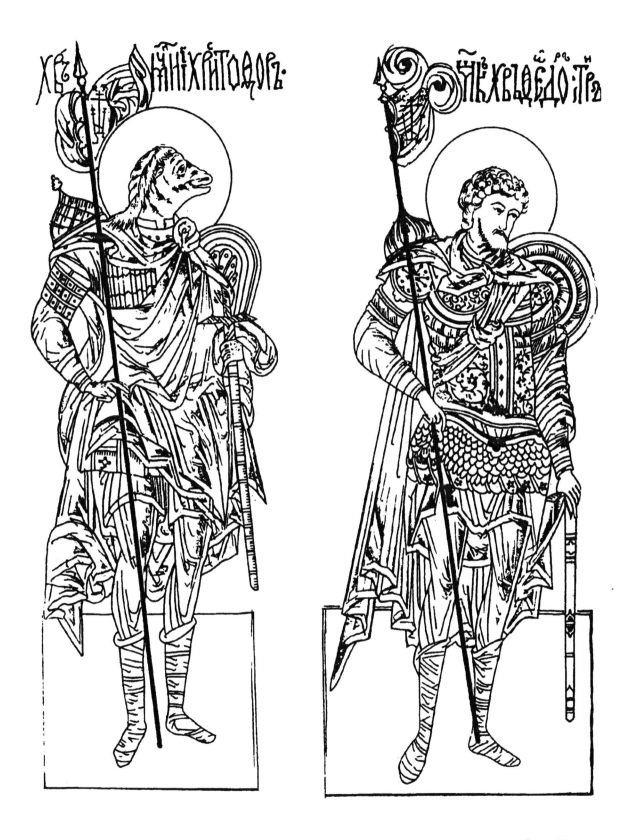

Sketch 51. Glorious Martyr Christopher | Martyr of Christ Theodore Tyro

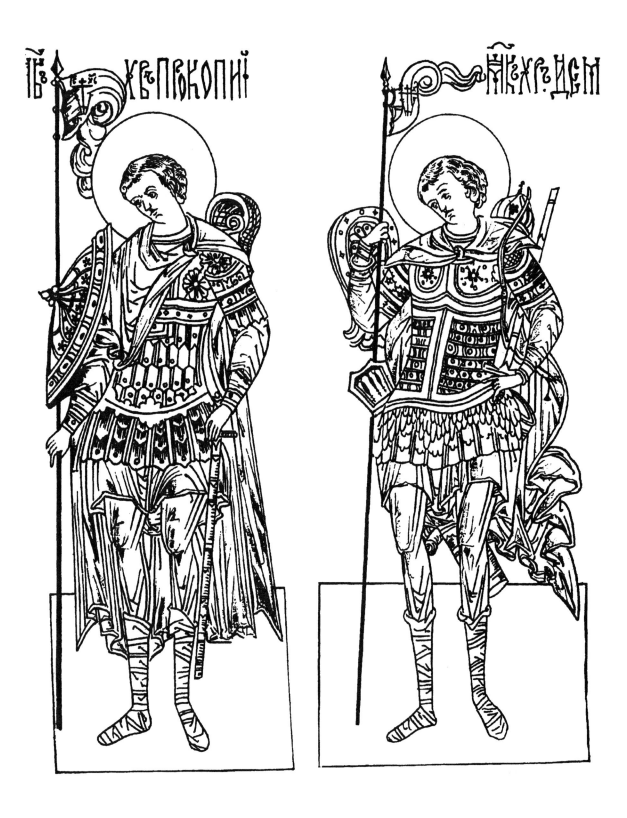

Sketch 52. Martyr of Christ Procopius | Glorious Martyr Demetrius

Sketch 53. Monastic Saint Sergius

Sketch 54. St. John the Theologian

Sketch 55. The Ascension of the Lord

Sketch 56. Emperor Constantine and Empress Helen

Sketch 57. John Chrysostom, Basil the Great,
Gregory the Theologian, Monastic St. Eudokia

Sketch 58. St. John the Forerunner

Sketch 59. St. Nicholas the Miracle Worker

Sketch 60. The Theophany

Sketch 61. St. John the Forerunner

Sketch 62. The Martyrdom of the holy Archdeacon Stephen

Sketch 63. St. Michael the Archangel

Sketch 64. St. Michael the Archangel

Sketch 65. The "Vladimir" Icon of the Mother of God

Sketch 66. St. John the Theologian

Sketch 67. The Protection of the Most Holy Theotokos

Sketch 68. St. Alexis the Man of God

Sketch 69. Ss. Michael and Gabriel, Archangels
Ss. Peter and Paul, Apostles

Sketch 70. The Washing of the Feet

Sketch 71. St. Mary Magdalene

Sketch 72. Jesus Christ "The Lord Immanuel"

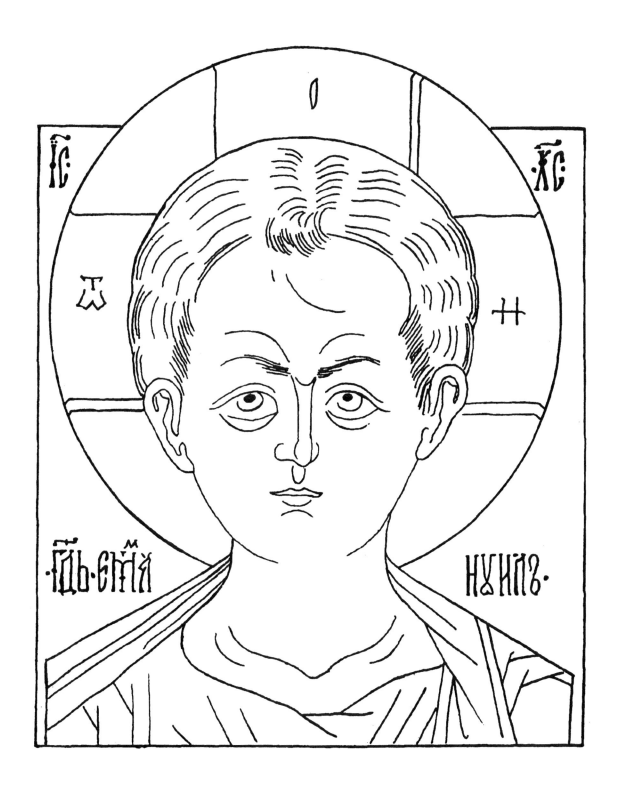

Sketch 73. Jesus Christ "The Lord "Immanuel"

Sketch 74. The Crucifixion

Sketch 75. The Nativity of Christ

Sketch 76. St. Nicholas the Miracle Worker

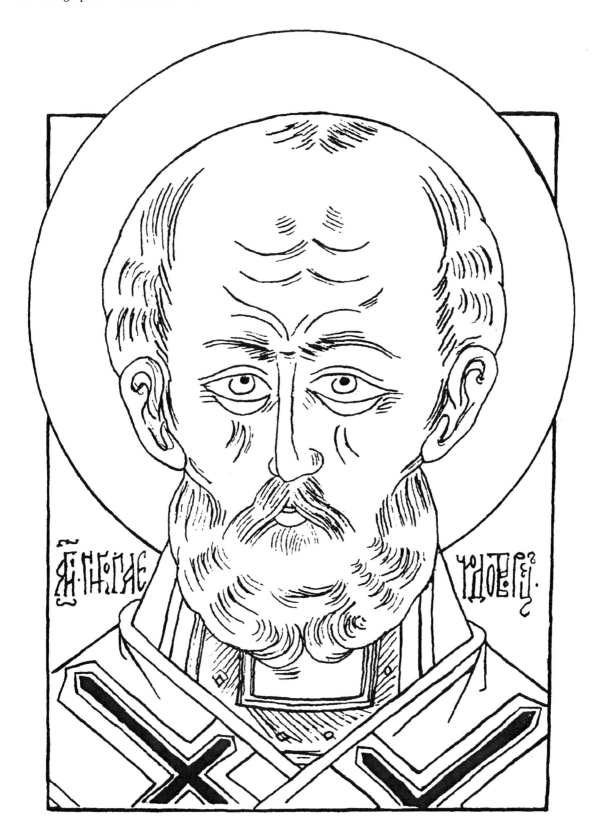

Sketch 77. St. Nicholas the Miracle Worker

Sketch 78. St. George the Victorious

Sketch 79. Jesus Christ "The Lord Almighty"

Sketch 80. Jesus Christ "The Savior"

Sketch 81. Ss. Boris and Gleb

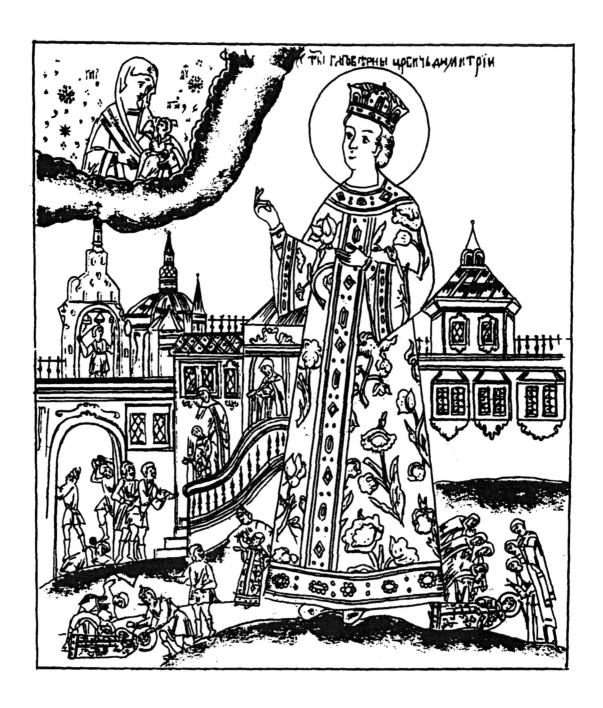

Sketch 82. St. Demetrius the Crown Prince

Sketch 83. St. John of the "Ladder"

Sketch 84. The Entry into the Temple

Sketch 85. The Holy Life-Creating Trinity

Sketch 86. The Nine Holy Martyrs in Cyzicus

Sketch 87. The Guardian Angel of the Human Soul

Sketch 88. The Monastic Saint Nicon

Sketch 89. The Monastic Saints Zosimas and Sabbatius

Sketch 90. Holy Hieromartyr Blaise

Antique Icons in the Collection of A. M. Postnikov, 1899

The authors, M. I. and V. I. Uspensky, dedicate this work to Professor Alfred Alexandrovich Parland as a token of their sincere and deep feelings of honor and respect.

LIST OF SKETCHES

Sketch 1. The All-Seeing Eye of God

Sketch 2. Jesus Christ "The Lord Almighty"

Sketch 3. Jesus Christ "The Lord Almighty"

Sketch 4. Jesus Christ "The Lord Almighty"

Sketch 5. Jesus Christ "The Lord Almighty"

Sketch 6. Jesus Christ "The Lord Almighty"

Sketch 7. Deisis

Sketch 8. The "Vladimir" Icon of the Mother of God

Sketch 9. The "Vladimir" Icon of the Mother of God

Sketch 10. The "Vladimir" Icon of the Mother of God

Sketch 11. The "Vladimir" Icon of the Mother of God

Sketch 12. The "Vladimir" Icon of the Mother of God

Sketch 13. The "Vologodsky" Icon of the Mother of God

Sketch 14. The Mother of God "Joy of All Who Sorrow"

Sketch 15. The Icon of the Mother of God "Of the Don"

Sketch 16. The Image of the Most Holy Theotokos "The Sign"

Sketch 17. The Icon of the Mother of God "Life Bearing Fountain"

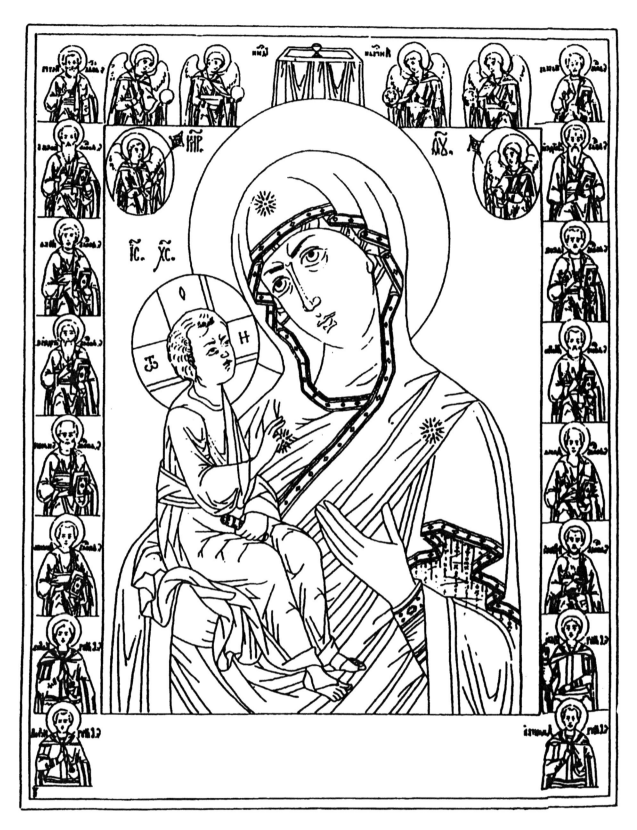

Sketch 18. The "Jerusalem" Icon of the Mother of God

Sketch 19. The "Kazan" Icon of the Mother of God

Sketch 20. The "Kazan" Icon of the Mother of God

Sketch 21. The "Kazan" Icon of the Mother of God

Sketch 22. The "Kazan" Icon of the Mother of God

Sketch 23. The Icon of the Mother of God "The Stone Not Cut By Hand"

Sketch 24. The "Kursk" Icon of the Mother of God

Sketch 25. The "Virgin Before Birth" Icon of the Mother of God

Sketch 26. The Icon of the Mother of God "Growth of Reason"

Sketch 27. The "Seven Lakes" Icon of the Mother of God

Sketch 28. The "Smolensk" Icon of the Mother of God

Sketch 29. The "Smolensk" Icon of the Mother of God

Sketch 30. The "Smolensk" Icon of the Mother of God

Sketch 31. The "Smolensk" Icon of the Mother of God

Sketch 32. The "Smolensk" Icon of the Mother of God

Sketch 33. The "Tykhvin" Icon of the Mother of God

Sketch 34. The "Sweet Sorrow" Icon of the Most Holy Theotokos

Sketch 35. The "Sweet Sorrow" Icon of the Most Holy Theotokos

Sketch 36. The "Theodore" Icon of the Mother of God

Sketch 37. The "Theodore" Icon of the Mother of God

Sketch 38. The "Theodore" Icon of the Mother of God

Sketch 39. The Mother of God and Hieromartyr Blaise

Sketch 40. Holy Prophet Elias

Sketch 41. Holy Prophet Elias

Sketch 42. Holy Prophet Elias

Sketch 43. St. John the Forerunner

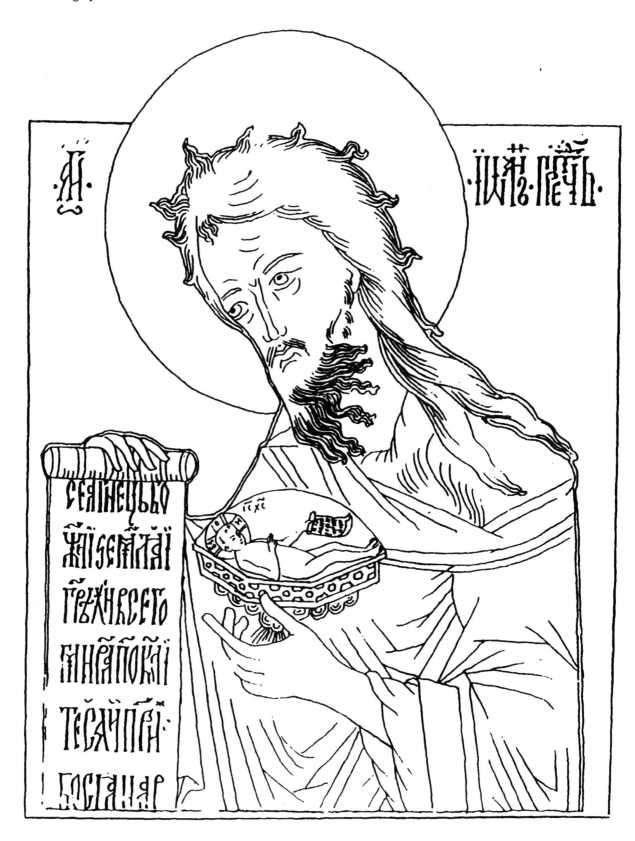

Sketch 44. St. John the Forerunner

Sketch 45. St. John the Forerunner

Sketch 46. The Twelve Apostles

Sketch 47. St. Nicholas the Miracle Worker

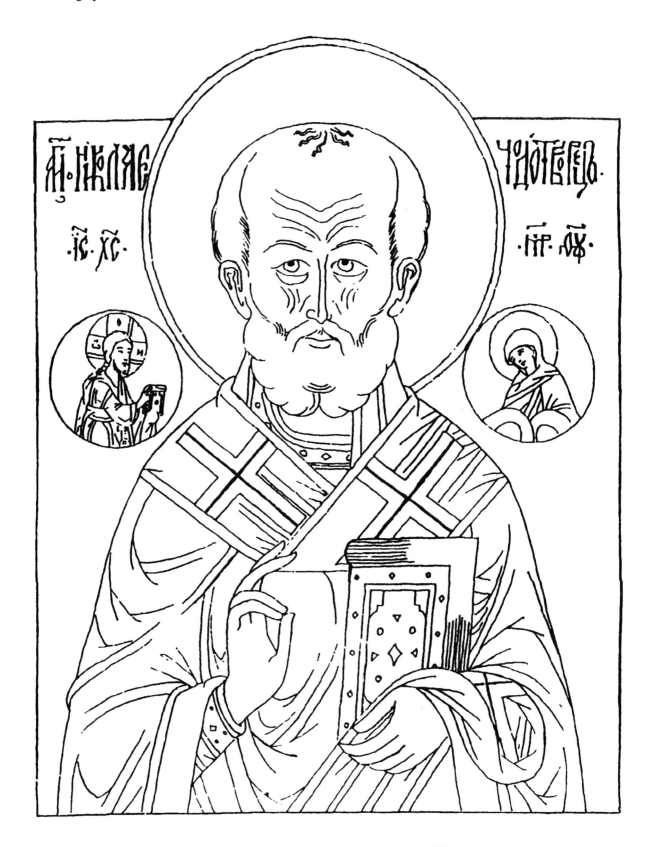

Sketch 48. St. Nicholas the Miracle Worker

Sketch 49. St. Nicholas Miracle Worker

Sketch 50. St. Nicholas Miracle Worker

Sketch 51. Miracle Workers of Moscow

Sketch 52. Miracle Workers of Moscow

Sketch 53. Miracle Workers of Moscow

Sketch 54. The Holy Protomartyr and Archdeacon Stephen

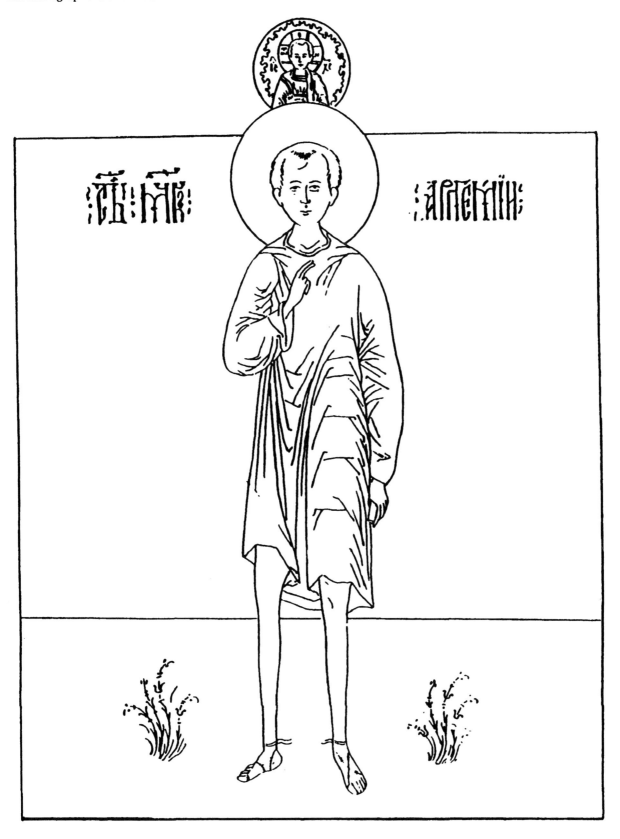

Sketch 55. Holy Martyr Artemius

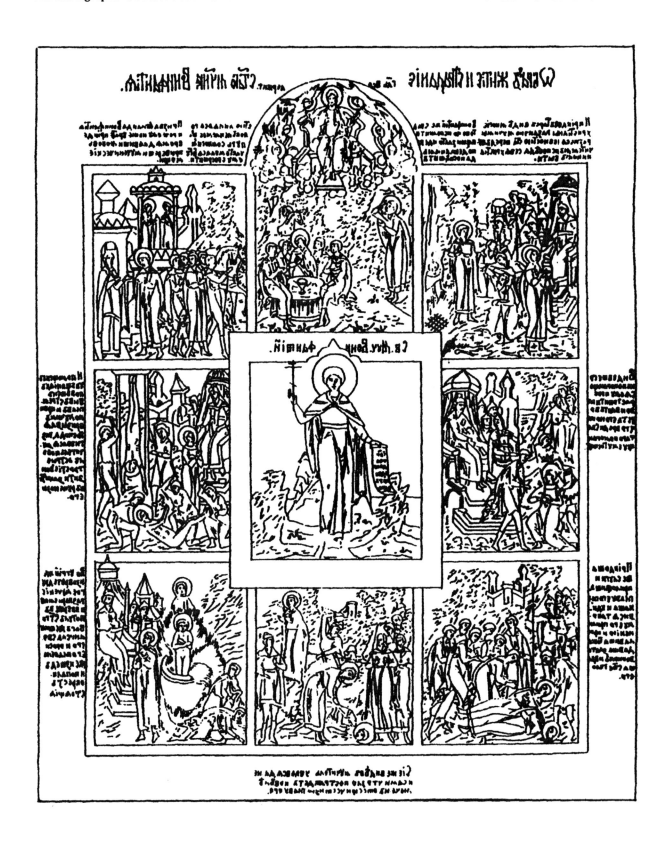

Sketch 56. Holy Martyr Boniface

Sketch 57. St. George the Victorious

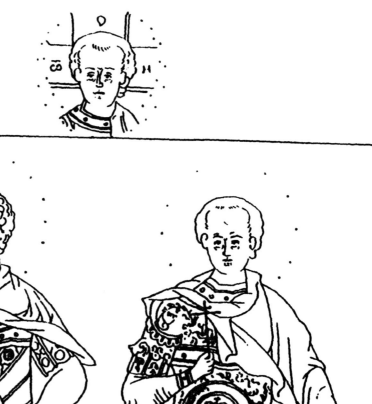

Sketch 58. St. George the Victorious and St. Demetrius of Thessalonica

Sketch 59. St. Demetrius of Thessalonica

Sketch 60. Holy Martyr Menas

Sketch 61. The Nine Holy Martyrs in Cyzicus and the Monastic St. Paisius

Sketch 62. Holy Martyr Thecla

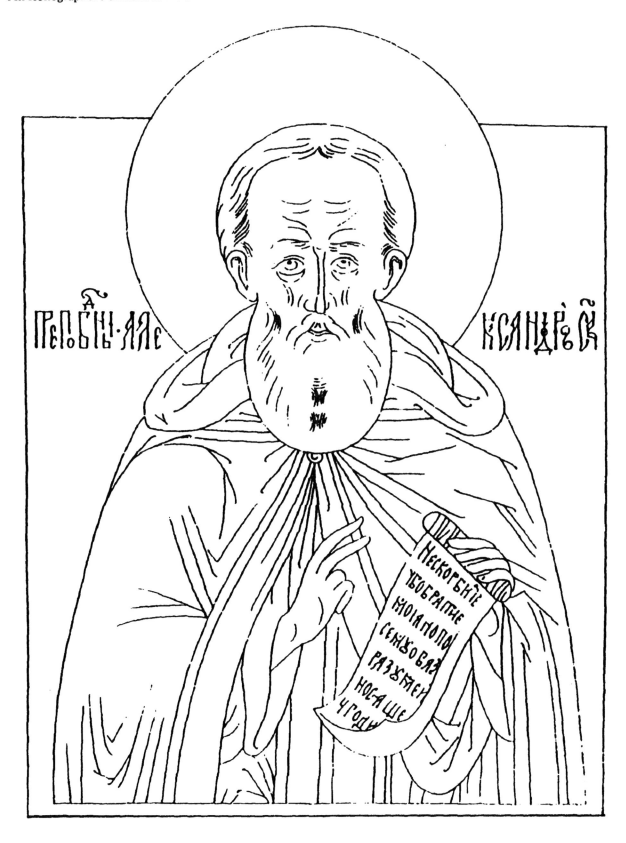

Sketch 63. Monastic St. Alexander of Svir

Sketch 64. St. Alexander of Svir

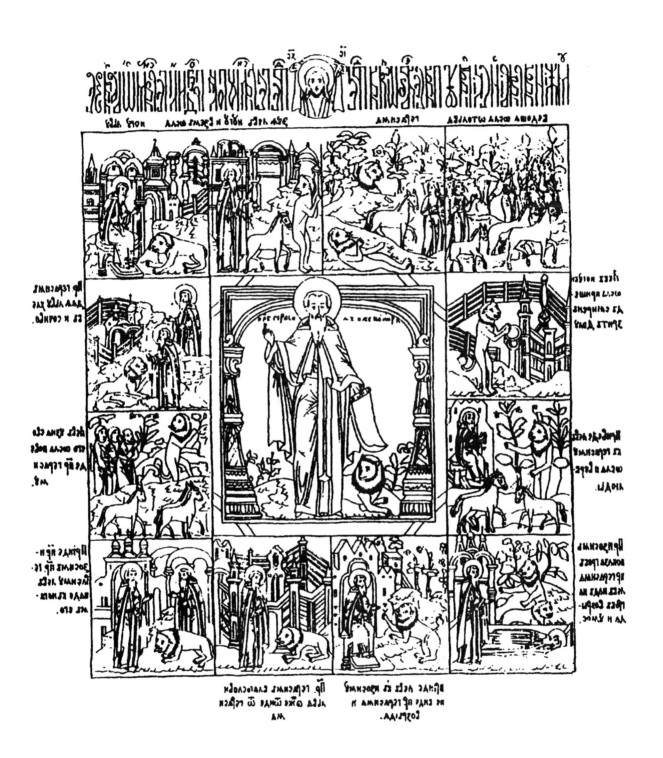

Sketch 65. Monastic St. Gerasimus

Sketch 66. Monastic Ss. Sabbas, Stephen and Martyr Sabinus

Sketch 67. Monastic Ss. Ephraim and Arcadius

Sketch 68. Monastic St. Jerome the Desert Dweller

Sketch 69. Miracle Workers of Novgorod

Sketch 70. St Artemius of Verkolesky

Sketch 71. Holy Princess Olga

Sketch 72. Holy Princes Vladimir, Boris and Gleb

Sketch 73. The Nativity of the Mother of God

Sketch 74. The Nativity of the Mother of God

Sketch 75. The Annunciation of the Mother of God

Sketch 76. The Annunciation of the Mother of God

Sketch 77. The Annunciation of the Mother of God

Sketch 78. The Annunciation of the Mother of God

Sketch 79. The Nativity of Christ

Sketch 80. The Nativity of Christ

Sketch 81. The Resurrection of Christ

Sketch 82. The Resurrection of Christ

Sketch 83. The Creation of the World

Sketch 84. The Creation of the World

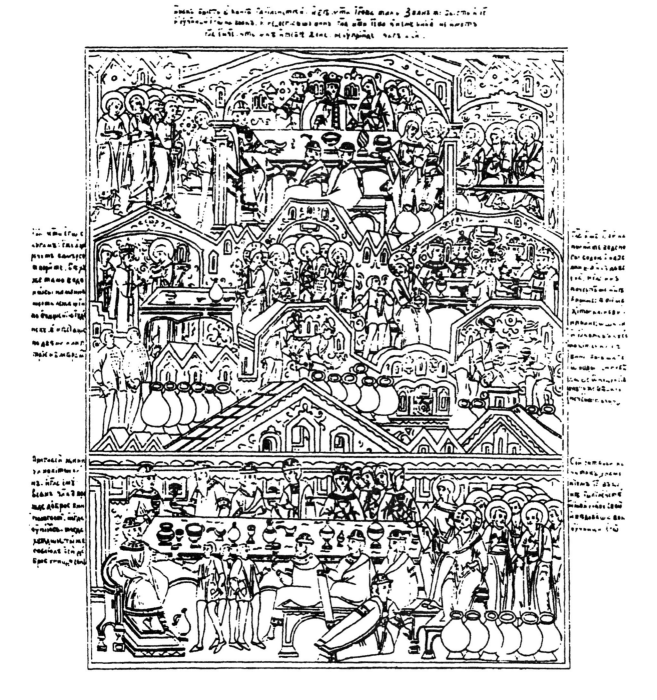

Sketch 85. The Marriage Feast in Cana

Sketch 86. The Crucifixion with the Evangelists

Sketch 87. The Appearance of the Mother of God Three Days
after the Dormition

Sketch 88. The Procession of the Venerable Wood of the Lord's Cross

Sketch 89. The Miracle of the Icon "The Sign of the Mother of God"

Sketch 90. The Vision of the Monastic St. Sergius

Sketch 91. "Let Everything That Has Breath Praise the Lord"

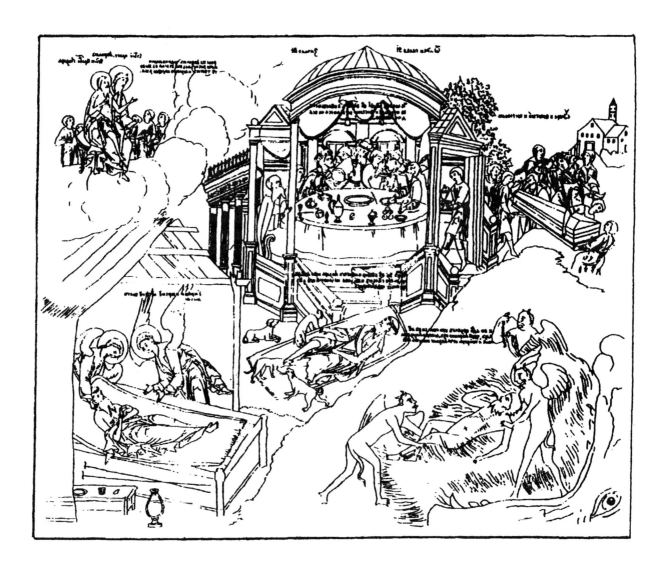

Sketch 92. The Parable of the Rich Man and Lazarus

Sketch 93. "Behold, the Lamb of God!"

Sketch 94. "Do Not Weep for Me, Mother"

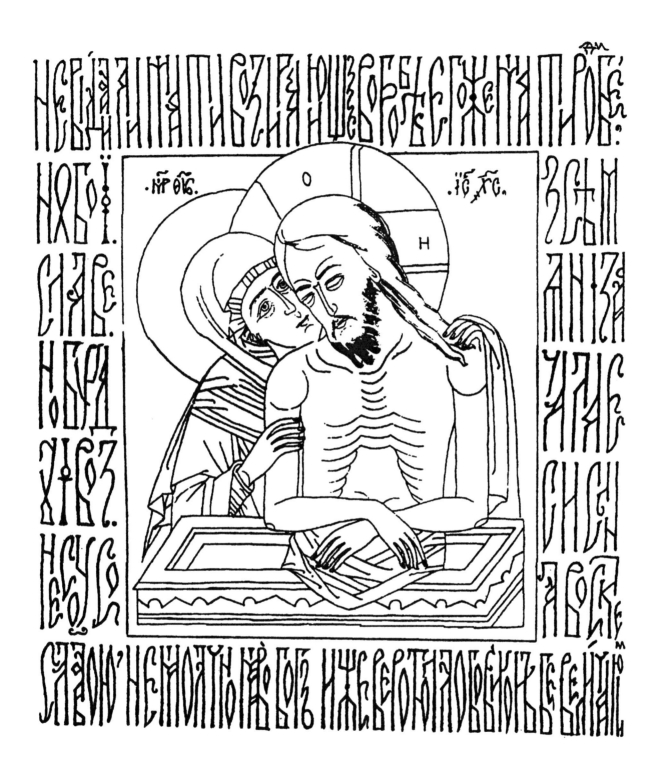

Sketch 95. "Do Not Weep For Me, Mother"

Sketch 96. "In You Rejoices"

Sketch 97. "Our Father"

Sketch 98. The Liturgy

GLOSSARY

Abyss A black crevasse or cave in an icon that may denote a hole in the ground or the underworld; i.e., hell or Hades.

Ancient of Days This is a title for God the Father in icons. Actually it seems that this Person is actually God the Son at times, for example, as a depiction of the Creator.

Angel of the Lord In the Old Testament our Lord Jesus Christ appeared a number of times in His Pre-incarnate Person called the "Angel of the Lord." The Angel of the Lord in this sense is the Second Person of the Holy Trinity and is always singular. He is not to be confused with an ordinary angel, also called an "angel of the Lord."

Apostles' robes The cloak (which appears more like a toga) and the tunic as worn by the Savior and the Apostles. Their tunics very often have a golden ornamental stripe called a "clavis" on the right shoulder down to the right ankle which distinguishes it from a martyr's tunic.

Bishops' cap This is not the high bulging miter of modern times, but a flat topped cloth hat with several sections sometimes ornamented with small icons. At times it is a triangular hat.

Blessed Translates the Slavonic word *"blazheny"* which generally denotes a saint who is not assigned to a certain category, e.g. "martyr." Thus in the Slavonic church books "Saint" Olga is literally "Blessed" Olga, but this does not diminish her sainthood in any way. (The term should not be confused with a stage of the canonization procedure in the Roman Catholic church.) More often it is the title for a "fool for Christ's sake," i.e., the saint feigned insanity and literally lived the words of the Gospel ignoring the opinions and sensitivities of society around him.

Clavis From the Latin word for "key." This was the stripe of nobility on ancient Roman togas and appears now as a golden stripe on apostles' tunics or a colored stripe on bishops' tunics.

Cloak This outer or upper garment has various forms depending on the life circumstances of a saint. It can resemble a toga, but it also can be a cape, especially as "martyrs' robes." The same word is used for a priest's or bishop's phelonion as well as a monastic mantle. The material piled up on a deacon's shoulder under the orarion is a cloak.

Church Slavonic This is the language of the modern printed church service books and is common to all Slavic Orthodox. It has been highly organized so that every letter and

A

accent mark distinguishes a case or number in grammar, or a word to avoid confusion. For example, the masculine adjective in the genitive case ends with _ᵃгⱳ and the accusative with _ᵃгⱺ; the root sounds the same, but the word ᴍи́рᶎ means "peace," ᴍі́рᶎ means "world," ᴍѵ́рⱺ means "chrism," and ᴍѷ́ры is St. Nicholas' city; singular, dual and plural numbers are distinguished by different forms of the letters ⱺ ⱳ, ꞓ ꞓ ѣ, and the circumflex accentˆ. Very little of this grammar is found in the Slavonic written on the icons, and almost none of it is found in modern Russian.

Cross patterned Describes the "polystaurion" or "many crosses" pattern (which may include circles, squares or angles) and is reserved to bishops. It may be painted on either a saccos or a phelon.

Deisis This comes from the Greek word δέησις which means "prayer". The icon usually shows the Mother of God and St. John the Forerunner with other saints standing in prayer before the central figure our Lord Jesus Christ. An angel deisis usually shows only the heads of Ss. Michael and Gabriel in prayer before the Christ Child.

Field This refers to one of several areas or separate "scenes" in an icon; it is not necessarily separated by lines. Sometimes the fields or scenes overlap or "flow into one another."

Hieromartyr A martyr who is ordained, usually a bishop.

Holy Used somewhere before a proper name is equal to "saint."

Holy Trinity The Divinity is shown as three Persons. The "Angel" Trinity has three angels, the "Fatherhood" has God the Father with the Christ Child on His lap with the Holy Spirit as a dove. The "New Testament" Trinity has God the Father and Jesus Christ as a grown Man with the Holy Spirit as a dove between Them. There is no consistency in the use of these words as technical terms.

Lord of Sabaoth The Lord "of hosts." Another name for God the Father.

Mandylion Another word for *"acheiropoietes - [image] made without hands."* This icon shows the face of our Lord Jesus Christ on a cloth sometimes held by angels. It is found frequently on the upper margin of an icon.

Monastic saint Translates the Slavonic technical term *"prepodobny,"* which literally means "most like [the ideal, Christ]." It can refer to any holy person as a saint in general. More specifically it denotes a monk or nun saint. It can be used together with "martyr."

Mountains The technical term for the fanciful landscape of hills and rugged terrain in icons and may have unusual trees, caves, ravines, crevices, etc.

Omophorion The "Y" shaped vestment reserved to bishops worn over the shoulders and hangs down in the front and back. In icons it is always white with three crosses, and perhaps three dots and horizontal stripes, unless specified otherwise, as in the icon of the Protection of the Mother of God, October 1.

Palaces The technical term for the fanciful exteriors of buildings before which events occur in iconography. They may be adorned with drapes, grills, canopies, etc.

Pantocrator There are many titles to honor our Lord Jesus Christ. This Greek word means "the Ruler of all," that is, "the Almighty."

Patternbook Translates the Slavonic word "podlinnik" and the Greek word "hermeneia." These are the traditional and anonymous iconographers' guides and handbooks. They are of two types: representational or figurative, that is, drawings of icons, (e.g. *An Iconographer's Patternbook: The Stroganov Tradition*); or prose descriptions of icons, recipes for artist materials, directions or procedures to execute an icon or decorate a church, and miscellaneous information. Like the icons, nothing is signed; no sources are given. The patternbooks are rarely referred to in the literature about icons, but they solve many problems about the consistency and integrity of Orthodox iconography. More information about patternbooks may be found in the "Introduction" to *The 'Painter's Manual' of Dionysius of Fourna*, translated by Paul Hetherington, printed and distributed by Oakwood Publications.

Phelonion The cloak-like vestment, also "phelon" in Slavonic, worn like a poncho by priests and bishops.

Russian This is the spoken and written language of the Russian people for hundreds of years. Some Church Slavonic grammar and spellings were retained until the Soviet regime. For example, the letters е and ѣ, и and і were distinguished, the Greek letters ѵ and ѳ were used in loan words, and a final consonant was followed by a ъ. This is now called the "old orthography" which is still found in reprinted editions of classic texts and some modern publications.

Saccos The bishops' vestment that resembles the deacons' sticharion or "dalmatic."

Savior This title is rarely placed on icons, but rather "The Lord Almighty." Russians like to use the title the "Savior" to refer to our Lord Jesus Christ. In these volumes "Savior" is considered equivalent to "The Lord Almighty" so that similar icons will not have different names.

Slavonic A generic word used in these volumes to denote the language used to inscribe icons. The iconographers copied the inscriptions from other icons or their patternbooks.

C

Otherwise they wrote phonetically resulting in various spellings. The icons have some variations still found in modern Ukrainian Catholic editions of Church Slavonic service books.

Synaxis Translates "*sobor,*" the technical term for the liturgical commemoration honoring one or more of the persons included in a feast day or the holy angels. For example, the "Synaxis of the Mother of God" gives special honor to the Theotokos on the day after Christmas. The word literally means "assembly" or "meeting" and can also mean a synod of bishops or a cathedral church building."

Tunic A long garment that extends from the feet up to the throat and to the wrists. It may be any color. Depending on the category of saint it may be understood as a cassock, a sticharion, a long shirt, etc. Bishops' tunics very often have contrasting colored stripes (clavis) running up from the bottom hem to the shoulder. It may also be a "middle garment" or "short tunic".

BIBLIOGRAPHY

Book of Akathists to our Saviour, the Mother of God, and Various Saints, Holy Trinity Monastery, Printshop of St. Job of Pochaev, Jordanville, New York, 1994.

[*Christian Hymns to the Most Holy Heavenly Queen, the Ever-virgin Mary, the Theotokos, Composed on the Pattern of the Psalms*, Moscow, 1883.] A modern reprint of Church Slavonic transliterated into Russian old orthography.

[Dyachenko, Priest Magister Gregory. *Complete Church Slavonic Dictionary*. Moscow, 1899] From Slavonic to Russian.

Kovalchuk, Archpriest Feodor S.,*Wonder-working Icons of the Theotokos*, translated and compiled from the Russian, Youngstown, Ohio, 1985.

[*Large Prayerbook*, Holy Trinity Monastery, Printshop of St. Job of Pochaev, 1964] In Church Slavonic.

Life of the Virgin Mary, the Theotokos, viewed and treated within the framework of Sacred Scriptures, Holy Tradition, Patristics and other ancient writings, together with the Liturgical and Iconographic Traditions of the Orthodox Church, written and Compiled by Holy Apostles Convert, 16975 Highway 306, Buena Vista, Colorado, 81211, 1989.

Melnick, Gregory. *An Icon Painter's Notebook: the Bolshakov Edition (An Anthology of Source Materials)* Oakwood Publications, 1995.

[*Miraculous Icons of the Mother of God in Russian History*, edited by Protodeacon Nikita Chakirov,] Russian Youth Committee, New York, 1976. In Russian.

Onasch, Konrad. *Icons*. A. S. Barns and Company, New York, 1963.

Orthodox Life, bi-monthly publication of the Brotherhood of St. Job of Pochaev at Holy Trinity Monastery, Jordanville, New York, 13361-0036.

[Poselyanin, E. ed. *Mother of God: a complete illustrated history of her earthly life and the miraculous icons sanctified by her name, St. Petersburg.*] No date, in Russian.

NKJ, The Holy Bible: The New King James Version. Thomas Nelson Publishers, Nashville, in many editions.

The Psalter According to the Seventy. Holy Transfiguration Monastery, Boston, Massachusetts, 1974.

Skorobucha, Heinz. *Maria: Russische Gnadenbilder* [Mary: Russian Miraculous Images] Verlag Aurel Bongers, Recklinghausen, 1967. In German

Timchenko, S. V. Russian Icons Today - Современная Православная Икона "Современник„ Moscow, 1994. In both Russian and English.

Velimirovic, Bishop Nikolai. *The Prologue from Ochrid: Lives of the Saints and Homilies for every day in the year*, trans. Mother Maria, Lazarica Press, Birmingham, 1986.

F

INDEX

H

1

CPSIA information can be obtained at www.ICGtesting.com
Printed in the USA
BVOW050902080513

320187BV00002B/6/P